GOODNIGHT DISGRACE

a play by Michael Mercer

Talonbooks   •   Vancouver   •   1986

copyright © 1986 Michael Mercer

published with assistance from the Canada Council

Talonbooks
201 1019 East Cordova Street
Vancouver
British Columbia   V6A 1M8
Canada

Typeset in Baskerville by Pièce de Résistance; printed and bound in Canada by Hignell Printing Ltd.

First printing September 1986

Canadian Cataloguing in Publication Data

Mercer, Michael, 1943–
    Goodnight disgrace

    A play.
    ISBN 0-88922-238-X

    1. Aiken, Conrad, 1889-1973, in fiction, drama, poetry, etc.   2. Lowry, Malcolm, 1909-1957, in fiction, drama, poetry, etc.   I. Title.
PS8576.E7G6 1986   C812'.54   C86-091454-2
PR9199.3.M47G6   1986

Preface

I still have the Penguin Modern Classics paperback of Lowry's
Under the Volcano that I bought in a Montreal bookstore over twenty
years ago. After countless readings, its pages are as limp as fabric
and have long ago worked their way out of the binding. Like
Lowry's ukulele in *Goodnight Disgrace*, it can't be played any more
but it's still good to hold. Here, if I ever took the time to puzzle
out the emphatic underlinings and scribbled marginalia, I would
probably find the original inspiration that led me to Cape Cod
and Conrad Aiken's front door in November, 1967.

It was crazy, and the sort of thing that only the young can be
forgiven for doing. I hadn't written or telephoned—chiefly because
a fellow writer working on a biography of T. S. Eliot had informed
me that Aiken was refusing all interviews. His health was failing
badly and he was preparing to return after a lifetime to Savannah,
Georgia to pass his remaining days. But I recklessly booted my
old station wagon down the Cranberry Highway, walked up to
the front door and told his wife I was a devoted fan of Malcolm
Lowry's and could I please speak to Conrad.

Even now, I can see him quite clearly, standing propped against
the kitchen sink, an old bathrobe tied across his paunch, responding
dreamily to my questions and casting a troubled glance, now and
again, out of the window where a chilly Atlantic wind was creating
chaos in the fallen leaves. Initially, he was quite reluctant to discuss
his relationship with Malcolm Lowry, pleading a memory enfeebled
by age. But through a long afternoon, he slowly warmed to the
subject and began to explore the past like someone jabbing a dying

fire with a poker, urging sparks into flame. Although I knew little at that point about what transpired between the two writers, there was something in Aiken's eyes—a disturbed compound of vitality and anguish—that prompted me to search out the details of what really happened. Much of it is recorded in Aiken's strangely beautiful autobiography, *Ushant*, and for those who take the trouble to check them, the events of *Goodnight Disgrace* are fundamentally factual. Aiken was indeed orphaned at twelve when his father shot his mother and then killed himself. At the age of forty, he did take on the young Lowry as a student, and was indeed urged by Malcolm's despairing father to take his profligate son on *in loco parentis*. There was a monumental fight in Grenada over Jan Gabriel, and another later in Mexico when Aiken discovered that Lowry was using some of his former master's material in his novel.

I must add, however, that this play was not created from any desire to record "real" events. It simply transpired that these "real" events needed little modification to bear the dramatic truth I was seeking. It would be more correct to say that the play is an act of exorcism, and even contrition. When I met Conrad Aiken in 1967, he was a Pulitzer Prize winning poet with four novels, a wealth of brilliant short stories and a lifetime's dedication to his craft behind him. And yet I had read not a word he had written. In the years following, I made up for this, and was so impressed by his talent that I sat down in 1973 and penned a thirty-page letter of appreciation to him. On the day that I mailed it to him, he died in a rest home in Savannah, Georgia, by report a highly embittered man liking only, as one of his obituary writers put it, "martinis, comic books and the fiction of John O'Hara." I had lost my chance forever of making amends to a very fine writer, and this, I believe, more than anything else provided the original motive to undertake the play. The first draft was written in fourteen feverish nights between eight at night and eight in the morning in 1977. I tucked it away in my cupboard with thoughts of returning to it one day, and there it might have remained, but for the egging, encouragement and invaluable assistance of my good and talented friend, Leon Pownall, who refused to leave me alone with my ghosts and did so much to give them breath and life again on the stage.

Michael Mercer
Vancouver, 1986

Goodnight Disgrace was first performed by the Shakespeare Plus Theatre Company in Nanaimo, British Columbia, on July 5, 1984, with the following cast:

Conrad Aiken	Matt Walker
Nurse	Sheri-D Wilson
Malcolm Lowry	Ron Halder
Clarissa Lorenz	June Mayhew
Arthur O. Lowry	Don Wallace
Ed Burra	Sam Mancuso
Jan Gabriel	Joelle Rabu

Directed by Leon Pownall
Codirected by Michael Fawkes
Set Designed by Neil Rutherford
Projected Paintings and Artwork by Paul Kuzma

Goodnight Disgrace was also performed at the Toronto Free Theatre, in co-production with The Shaw Festival, in Toronto, in March 1985, with the following cast:

Conrad Aiken	Matt Walker
Nurse	Carole Galloway
Malcolm Lowry	Geraint Wyn Davies
Clarissa Lorenz	Wendy Thatcher
Arthur O. Lowry	Ron Hartmann
Ed Burra	David Schurmann
Jan Gabriel	Caroline Yeager

Directed by Leon Pownall
Set Designed by Diz Marsh
Projected Paintings and Artwork by Paul Kuzma

Goodnight Disgrace was also performed by the Shakespeare Plus Theatre Company in Nanaimo, British Columbia, in July 1985, with the following cast:

Conrad Aiken	Graeme Campbell
Nurse	June Mayhew
Malcolm Lowry	Ron Halder
Clarissa Lorenz	Gabriel Rose
Arthur O. Lowry	Barrie Baldaro
Ed Burra	Richard Newman
Jan Gabriel	Joelle Rabu

Directed by Leon Pownall
Set Designed by Neil Rutherford
Projected Paintings and Artwork by Paul Kuzma

Goodnight Disgrace was also performed at the Playhouse Theatre in Vancouver, in September 1985, with the following cast:

Conrad Aiken	Graeme Campbell
Nurse	June Mayhew
Malcolm Lowry	Ron Halder
Clarissa Lorenz	Gabriel Rose
Arthur O. Lowry	Barry Baldero
Ed Burra	Richard Newman
Jan Gabriel	Joelle Rabu

Directed by Leon Pownall
Set Designed by Terry Bennett
Projected Paintings and Artwork by Paul Kuzma

ACT ONE

Although the play can be staged in a variety of ways, the fluid movement from scene to scene would suggest a fundamentally non-realistic presentation, employing a minimum of props. The original production was performed on a slightly raked stage painted black, with a simple table and three chairs, also black, that remained throughout. Six rear-screen projection surfaces were at the back of the stage, configured in two rows of three, one above the other. Only in certain scenes were all screens used simultaneously; others used three, four or five in a variety of geometric configurations. The visual content of the slides was coloured photographs of non-representational paintings by Vancouver artist Paul Kuzma.

Scene One

A rest home, Savannah, Georgia—1973.

Music: Don Maclean's "American Pie."

Projected rear-screen images provide the impression of the antiseptic interior of a rest home, shadowed in the early evening.

CONRAD AIKEN is wheeled on stage by the NURSE, who pushes his wheelchair into a position facing the audience. She fusses with the angle as if trying to align his view through an imaginary window.

AIKEN is a man of 85, wrapped in an old bathrobe, and with a bandage on his head. He appears tired and embittered.

NURSE: *pointing*
Look. There's the moon. Just coming up. Now you watch it...and I'll be right back.   *hesitating*   Now don't go away.

It's an old rest home joke, and he's heard it far too often. AIKEN gazes out over the audience.

The NURSE exits.

AIKEN speaks after a long moment of thought.

AIKEN:
And I ask: where am I? A voice comes back to me, presently, and says: Savannah. Savannah, Georgia. Then I smell it again in the darkness... the place where I was born. I hear it again. The muddy Thunderbolt River where I fished with bamboo pole and bent pin. The wind in the skirts of the pine about the decaying

8

graveyard where we played so innocently at ghosts and goblins. For one moment...one beautiful moment... I think: I am back. I am beginning again. Beginning. Then. I feel. My bones grinding at the joints like drifts of polar ice, and I know the truth. This is not the beginning, and I am an old man freezing to death in a southern summer.

He leans back in the chair, defeated, and pulls the bathrobe more tightly around him, as the NURSE returns pushing a trolley freighted with kidney pans, scissors, disinfectant, and fresh dressings. She takes the scissors and prepares to cut the old dressing off his head.

NURSE:
My, my, I must say you cut quite a dashing figure with that bandage. Like the revolutionary soldier marching along with the flute.   *Beat.*   Or was it a drum?

AIKEN turns away, annoyed with the chatter.

You know, you've really upset the poor woman in the next room. That was very cruel of you, Mr. Aiken. Shame on you. She just wanted you to autograph one of your books of poetry for her. I should think you'd be flattered.

MALCOLM LOWRY enters carrying a suitcase and a ukulele. He sings a bawdy song as he up ends the suitcase, opens it, takes out a mickey of gin, and then sits on the suitcase studying AIKEN with amusement.

LOWRY appears as AIKEN first knew him: a drunken, rambunctious student of 19, looking young and very collegiate.

AIKEN: *absently quoting*
"An agreeable maker of coloured mists!"

NURSE:
Oh, isn't that lovely! Did you write that?

AIKEN:
It damn well isn't lovely! Aldous Huxley wrote
it.   *Beat.*   About me!

NURSE:
Keep your head still.

AIKEN:
Coloured mists, my ass!

NURSE:
Whoever this Huxley is, I'm sure he doesn't know more
about poetry than our Governor Carter. He made you
Poet Laureate of Georgia, didn't he?

AIKEN:
Oh, leave me alone woman!

> *LOWRY laughs, strums a chord on the ukulele and looks
> at AIKEN shaking his head. AIKEN stares at him in
> horror, then tries to clear the vision from his mind.*

to LOWRY   Get out of here!

NURSE:
Now be patient. Just a little longer.

LOWRY: *singing to tune of "Molly Malone"*
The voyage is over,
The circle complete.
Your mind is as worn
As the shoes on your feet.

> *He strums and takes a drink.*

speaking now   Poor old bird. This isn't the way you
imagined it, is it? Coming home. The final bankruptcy.

10

AIKEN tries to turn his head away as the NURSE is cleaning his wound.

NURSE:
Keep still, Mr. Aiken! It'll just sting for a moment.

LOWRY: *singing again*
Your ship nears the harbour,
Your landfall is found;
Your wake dies behind you,
Just a scroll of faint sound.

AIKEN:
What do you want of me?!

NURSE:
You should join the others in the day room. Play cards. Watch television or something. You're being very naughty, you know. Shut up in here all the time. *Beat.* Mr. Aiken?

LOWRY takes another swat at the bottle, and shakes his head at the memory. Warming himself with it.

LOWRY:
You'll never know how long it took me to build up the courage to meet you. *holding up the bottle* Dutch at that, old boy.

AIKEN:
Don't tell me about it.

NURSE:
I suppose you're right. Not much to watch, is there? It's all Watergate these days. Such a tragedy. Poor President Nixon. It's always the innocent who suffer most.

LOWRY:
Six times I stood in front of your door...the first five...I scurried away terrified. Must have done every bar in a ten-mile radius. *laughing* Made the mistake of

11

hitting the same one twice. The bartender says to me: *mimicking an American accent* "Yeah, I 'member. Straight gin. Look kid, how old are ya?" Nineteen. "Yer too damn young to be drinkin' the way you do." And then in that incomprehensible, absolutely paradoxical American way, he shoved another glass at me and said: "G'wan kid, have another. On the house."

The bandage is off and the NURSE looks closely, kneading the scalp line with her fingers. AIKEN chuckles at LOWRY.

NURSE:
What's so funny, Mr. Aiken?

LOWRY:
At that moment, I prayed fervently that God was a Yank, emptied the glass and came to see you.

The NURSE notices a scar on the other side of AIKEN'S head and moves to get a closer look. AIKEN stares absently off into space.

NURSE:
Mr. Aiken? You all right? *Pause.* That's strange. You've got another scar here.

AIKEN: *responding to NURSE*
In the shape of a cross.

NURSE: *looking closely*
A little cross. *Beat.* I don't recall anything about this in your medical record.

LOWRY stands and spreads his arms in greeting.

LOWRY: *acting out meeting*
"Conrad! I'd know you anywhere!" *Beat.* Of
course I would. Your photo was on the back of the
novel. And then I was so nervous. Or drunk. Or both.
I forgot to introduce myself. And you said...

AIKEN:
Who the hell are you?! *to Nurse* It doesn't
matter. It happened a long time ago.

NURSE:
At your age, Mr. Aiken, everything matters. Was it
another concussion?

AIKEN:
A cracked skull. *Beat.* For pity's sake! Leave me
alone! Let me die in peace!!

NURSE: *long suffering sigh*
Very well. We'll leave this open to the air. But I'm
going to redress it before you go to bed.

*The NURSE gathers things on the table as LOWRY
returns to his suitcase, takes out a dumb-bell, and exercises
with it.*

LOWRY:
Requiescat in pace. *Beat.* A luxury, I fear, not
afforded to the likes of you and me, old
boy. *Pause.* Well? Are you ready?

The NURSE turns as she is about to leave.

*LOWRY puts the dumb-bell back in the suitcase and takes
a toilet seat out. He turns back to AIKEN.*

13

NURSE: *returning*
I feel I must mention this, Mr. Aiken. Some of our other residents have been...well...mentioning that you've been talking aloud at night. And it's disturbing them. If you're having difficulty sleeping, we can provide a sedative, if you wish.

AIKEN stares at the toilet seat with amusement, heightened by the fact that LOWRY is suggestively placing it behind the NURSE as she speaks to AIKEN. The NURSE hovers for a moment for an answer, but soon realizes that she is not going to get a sensible response. She sighs with exasperation and exits pushing the wheeled trolley ahead of her.

LOWRY holds the toilet seat to one side, picks a quotation from the air after a moment of thought, and throws it to AIKEN.

LOWRY: *quoting*
"Ah, God! What trances of torments does that man endure who is consumed with unachieved desire. He sleeps with clenched hands; and wakes with his own bloody nails in his palms."   *pointing to AIKEN*
Ah? Ah?

AIKEN:
Melville. What the hell else could you ever quote but *Moby Dick*?

LOWRY:
The works of Conrad Aiken.

AIKEN:
Don't persecute me! I'm an old man...with nowhere to go. You understand? NOWHERE!

LOWRY: *studying toilet seat*
I wonder how many accumulated days of our lives we
spend perching on these things? Bloody hard, old boy,
to discuss the relative demerits of eternity with a toilet
seat in your hands.

AIKEN:
What do you want of me? What?!

LOWRY:
Teach me. Please. Teach me.

AIKEN:
NO..! NO..! Go away!!

> *LOWRY gets into a wrestler's crouch and holds the toilet
> seat out towards AIKEN.*

LOWRY:
Come on. Once again. Youth against experience. Eh?
Come on, old bird. Don't be timid. Rush headlong into
the darkness with me. "Art requires the ultimate
sacrifice." Remember that one? Or where you just
spewing out intellectual bullshit to impress me?

> *AIKEN raises himself to his feet. He staggers slightly and
> finds his balance. Then, before the audience, the years fall
> away from him. He moves around behind the wheelchair,
> discarding his bathrobe with the years, and comes forward
> to meet LOWRY as a man, again, of 40.*

> *LOWRY braces himself to wrestle.*

You want to fight, old man? I'll give you a fight!

> *AIKEN charges LOWRY. They wrestle. LOWRY
> throws AIKEN, who then trips up LOWRY and grabs
> the toilet seat. LOWRY helps AIKEN into the wheelchair,
> and pushes him off-stage. The two of them are exultant.*

Blackout.

Musical Bridge: Opening few bars of the Charleston.

Scene Two

Aiken's apartment, Cambridge, Massachusetts—1929.

CLARISSA "JERRY" LORENZ enters and after studying the disarray of the room for a moment she puts the table upright (over the toilet seat) and places the chairs in position at the table.

CLARISSA is a striking woman in her 30s, dressed in a business-like fashion for the 1920s.

CLARISSA:
   Conrad?   *Pause.*   Conrad?

There is the sound of a toilet flushing off-stage, and AIKEN enters. He is a man of 40, and has a bandage around his head as in the first scene. He is suffering the combined agonies of a cracked skull and a monumental hangover.

AIKEN:
   Hi, Jerry. How was New York?

CLARISSA:
   What the hell's been going on here?

AIKEN:
   The editor liked your article, didn't he?

CLARISSA: *noticing the bandage*
For God's sake! What's happened?

AIKEN:
The cheque? You got the cheque?

CLARISSA:
Yes! Yes, I got the cheque. Now will you tell me why
you've got a bandage on your head?

AIKEN:
Malcolm.

CLARISSA:
Malcolm?

AIKEN:
The English boy I'm tutoring for the summer.

CLARISSA:
What are you teaching him? Brain surgery?

AIKEN:
Oh, it's nothing. A cracked skull, that's all.

CLARISSA:
A cracked skull! For pity's sake, Conrad!

AIKEN:
I slipped and hit the fireplace. Could happen to anyone.

CLARISSA:
You were drunk, I take it.

AIKEN:
No. I wouldn't say that. If you want to be a demon for
accuracy, absolutely stinking pissed to the gills.

AIKEN pulls CLARISSA down on his lap.

CLARISSA:
You look like hell, you know.

AIKEN:
Hey, you want to see my scar? It's in the shape of a little cross.

CLARISSA:
How handy for seducing nuns!

AIKEN:
I have a more interesting habit in mind, my dear.

CLARISSA:
Conrad! You've got a hangover.

AIKEN:
True.

CLARISSA:
A cracked skull.

AIKEN:
Equally true.

CLARISSA:
And you still want sex!

AIKEN:
I don't *want* sex, Jerry. I desperately *need* sex. There's a huge difference, you know.

CLARISSA:
Where's this Malcolm?

AIKEN:
I sent him to the store.

CLARISSA: *standing up*
Conrad! Is this boy going to Cape Cod with us?

AIKEN:
   Yes.

CLARISSA:
   We could have had the whole summer together alone.
   And now we have a boarder.

AIKEN:
   Sorry. Malcolm's old man is putting up sixty dollars a
   week for this, Jerry. I need it for the alimony and child
   support.

CLARISSA:
   You can't stand teaching during the winter, and now
   you give away our summer together....

AIKEN:
   This is different.

CLARISSA:
   Who said to me: "I'm sick to death of showing a bunch
   of Harvard pukes how to spell their goddamn double-
   barrelled names with the goddamn hyphens in the right
   place!" Who?

AIKEN:
   Harvard pukes, Jerry! Harvard pukes!

CLARISSA:
   You shouldn't *have* to tutor. Damn it, you're one of the
   best writers in this country!

AIKEN:
   AND middle-aged, AND nearly destitute. AND, if it
   needs any more ANDS...   *Beat.*   ...there's only
   two of us in the whole damn world who share that
   opinion.

CLARISSA:
   Nonsense!

AIKEN:

Make it three.   *Beat.*   Malcolm came all the way
from England to study with me. You'll like him, Jerry.
Really. He's got promise, truly. It's a little early to
say... I've only glanced at his work...but I can feel it.
He's got something in him. Major key.

CLARISSA:

Conrad, be careful. Just because he drinks and makes a
perfect playmate for you, doesn't make him a great
writer.

AIKEN:

He has this thing about coincidences. He reads them as
signs. Portents. The working of dark fates. He believes I
dedicated *Blue Voyage* to him on some strange astral
plane. I swear he knows the novel by heart.

CLARISSA:

I seem to remember you dedicated that book to me.

AIKEN.

I just used your initials. C.M.L. Strange coincidence.
They're his too. Clarence Malcolm Lowry. Proof to
him, that the fates ordained he study writing with me.

CLARISSA:

You're serious about this.

AIKEN:

Jerry, the moment he walked in the door...I can't
explain it. I felt a kinship with him. A
spiritual...sympathy.

CLARISSA:

Speaking of spiritual sympathy...what's the toilet seat
doing under the table?

AIKEN:

The toilet seat's under the table?

CLARISSA:
Yes, I'd say so. Definitely under the table.

AIKEN:
It shouldn't be there.

CLARISSA:
No kidding.

AIKEN:
Definitely not. That's where Malcolm sleeps.

CLARISSA:
Under the table?!

AIKEN:
He says it reminds him of a ship's bunk. He loves the sea, you know.

CLARISSA:
Does he always sleep with a toilet seat under the table?

AIKEN:
Not any more he doesn't! The toilet seat is my trophy. From now on it sleeps with me.

CLARISSA:
I hope you'll be very happy together. Conrad, you mean the two of you were fighting over a toilet seat?

AIKEN:
No!   *Beat.*   Wrestling, I guess you'd call it.

CLARISSA:
You cracked your skull wrestling over a toilet seat?

AIKEN:
The principle of the toilet seat, Jerry.   *Beat.*   You should have seen it. I hugged it all the way to the hospital. Malcolm with a worried arm around me. Me with the toilet seat.

CLARISSA:
Don't you care about your reputation?

AIKEN:
Nobody recognized me, no fear! Even after I gave my name, they didn't know who I was. "Mr. Acheing" the nurse insisted on calling me. "Now Mr. Acheing, why don't you let me hold your toilet seat while the doctor fixes you up.

LOWRY: *off-stage—singing over dialogue*
One white one
One black one
And one with a little shite one
And the hair of his dicky-di-do
Hung down to his knees.

AIKEN:
Malcolm!...Now give him a chance. For me. And don't mention last night. He got up this morning mortified with guilt. Like a punished puppy.

LOWRY enters singing the opening bars of Bessie Smith's "Downhearted Blues." He is visibly drunk.

CLARISSA:
Cute!

LOWRY collapses into a chair and appears in a vague stupor. AIKEN goes over to him.

AIKEN:
Malcolm? Good morning, Malcolm. Malcolm?

LOWRY: *recovering*
Home from the sea, old bird...with not one, but two unbroken virgins. Gin and vermouth.   *holding up the bottles he is carrying*   Unbroken! Which is a miracle considering how many times I fell over walking back.   *He turns and sees CLARISSA.*   Oh dear!

22

CLARISSA:
Good Lord!

Blackout.

Musical Bridge: Opening bars of "Old Cape Cod."

Scene Three

A room in a Cape Cod cabin—1929.

LOWRY strums on his ukulele as AIKEN paces the floor studying a manuscript.

LOWRY: *singing*
Ain't got no money,
Ain't got a cent,
Can't pay the butcher,
Can't pay the rent.

AIKEN:
Malcolm, put that damned ukulele down and come here.

LOWRY:
This isn't a ukulele. It's called a taropatch.

AIKEN: *trying to maintain calm*
A taropatch.

LOWRY:
Yes, but it's an honest mistake. It *looks* like a ukulele.

AIKEN:

> In that case, can you put the damned taropatch
> down?! *waving manuscript at him* What the hell's
> this supposed to be?

LOWRY:

> Oh that. It's the scene in my novel that comes two after
> the one I was reading you yesterday.

AIKEN:

> And where's the one that comes before this, and after
> the one that you were reading me yesterday?

LOWRY:

> I was afraid you'd ask that. I seem to have misplaced it.

AIKEN:

> Think you can find it, Malc? I mean, I'm dying to
> know why two characters have suddenly developed
> injured arms, and a third has sadly moved on to the
> past tense.

LOWRY:

> As a matter of fact, I've changed my mind about that.
> It all comes out.

AIKEN:

> So glad you told me.

LOWRY:

> Conrad...it's a dream of mine to write a novel like
> yours. A novel in which absolutely nothing happens.

AIKEN:

> I'm thrilled you liked it. *Beat.* Malc, you're
> writing about the sea. For God's sake learn from the
> sea! Ebb and flow.

LOWRY:

> Ebb and flow...

AIKEN:
>...some brilliant description...but you can't sustain an
entire novel on this...murky, introspective tone. All ebb.
No flow.

LOWRY:
>Needs a peppering of dialogue, does it?

AIKEN:
>For a start.   *Beat.*   Read through my novel...look
for it. Contraction, expansion. In, out, in, out. And
your adverbs....

LOWRY:
>What's wrong with my adverbs?

AIKEN:
>Individually, not a damn thing. But it's beyond me why
you have to line up six in a row to describe everything
from sunset to seagull shit!   *handing him the*
papers   From now on read everything aloud. You'll
hear it.

LOWRY: *reciting*
>"But in his heart he knew himself to be afraid..."

AIKEN:
>Louder!

LOWRY:
>"...afraid of living..."

AIKEN:
>Louder!

LOWRY:
>"Afraid of manhood..."

AIKEN:
>LOUDER!

LOWRY:

"AFRAID OF MANHOOD!"

LOWRY throws the manuscript over his shoulder.

AIKEN:

The task of the artist is to reach out and reclaim the unconscious. *Beat.* It's like walking down a street. You pass a house. And from an open window, you hear a windblown fragment of a beautiful orchestral movement you've never heard before. It's haunting. It's mysterious. It's magnificent. You desperately want to hear the whole thing. But you can't. *Beat.* The artist is the person who then sits down and attempts to reconstruct the entire symphony from that one, momentary fragment. It's an act of imagination. An act of creating a bridge from the unconscious to the conscious.

LOWRY:

And consciousness warrants the ultimate sacrifice.

AIKEN:

God! That's utterly brilliant! You just make that up?

LOWRY:

You said it. Last week.

AIKEN:

No wonder it's so brilliant. *Beat.* Are you keeping notes on me?

LOWRY:

Quite consciously, Conrad.

AIKEN:

Well, remember this. You've got to create a bridge from the unconscious to the conscious. Concentrate on the ebb and flow. Contraction and expansion. In. Out. In....

LOWRY breaks into a reverie.

LOWRY:

...out past the sputtering gasfire in the dining-room and beyond the wide French doors at the back of the house...I remember the garden. It was the richest garden I've ever seen...a world of tangible mysteries. A tree of heaven climbed up against the sky like a crack in a window pane. The pansies dissolved at a touch, the snapdragons yawned at a pinch, and the lily-of-the-valley brushed my palm like dried peas. In my childish curiosity, I would go out there with a table knife stolen from the kitchen drawer, and dig in the rich black loam. Under the earth, I found animal bones. Used as fertilizer, I imagine. As a child will do...I sniffed them. They smelled so unlike anything I had ever smelled before. Sour. Decaying. And yet oddly rich. It stirred something in me. Carried me beyond that garden and down to the Cast Iron shores, where huge freighters churned up the Mersey River stinking of tar and cabbages...and beyond, into the immense vacuum of the great North Atlantic, where other lands waited...teeming with life and the rank smells of humanity.   *Beat.* That's what an artist is to me. A child digging for bones in a garden.   *Pause.*   By the way, Conrad, how's your manuscript coming along?

AIKEN: *rising out of a trance*
Oh....I normally don't write more than four words a day.   *Beat.*   I usually get stuck on the third.

LOWRY:
I can save you hours of work, old bird. I've got the fourth.

AIKEN:
A bloody adverb?

LOWRY:
A noun.

27

AIKEN:
   Solid?

LOWRY:
   Liquid.

AIKEN:
   Martini?

LOWRY:
   Martini!

AIKEN:
   It's not time!

LOWRY:
   It feels like bloody time!

AIKEN:
   Tempt me.   *Beat.*   Denotation?

LOWRY:
   Extra dry, eleven to one, up with a twist, and cold as a
   publisher's heart.

AIKEN:
   And the connotation?

LOWRY:
   It connotes: dreaming evenings, crushed ice for stars,
   and warm sea currents of convivial conversation.

AIKEN:
   Are the metaphors mixed?

LOWRY:
   Well...actually...no. They're waiting for your age and
   experience.

AIKEN:

    Damn you, Lowry! You can't even mix a martini! You come in here...you steal my ideas...my time...

LOWRY:

    ...your knowledge...

AIKEN:

    ...my knowledge...

LOWRY:

    ...your images...

AIKEN:

    Damn right, boy! On the subject of that theft, I want those out of your manuscript immediately. I said go through my novel, but not with a tracing paper!

LOWRY:

    Imitation, they say, is the highest form of flattery.

AIKEN:

    Imitation! Imitation! You're trying to take possession, Lowry!

LOWRY:

    I've been giving that a lot of thought. It's a metaphysical problem. How can the Son of God become God?

        AIKEN is struck deeply by some underlying suggestion in the question, and for a moment sits in a disturbed silence. Finally he shakes himself out of it.

AIKEN:

    Simply. By transcending his earthly ignorance and learning the miracle of the martinis. Watch.

AIKEN takes the bottle of gin, opens it, and indicates that LOWRY do the same with the bottle of vermouth.
AIKEN takes a mouthful of gin and holds it without swallowing while indicating that LOWRY do the same with the vermouth. Then AIKEN gives LOWRY the gin, and he takes the bottle of vermouth. AIKEN adds a swig of vermouth to the gin that he is holding in his mouth, and LOWRY follows suit with the bottle of gin. AIKEN indicates that LOWRY keep the liquid mixture in his mouth, and slosh it around to blend the gin and vermouth. He swallows it, and LOWRY does the same.

Got an olive?

Blackout.

Scene Four

A beach, Cape Cod, Mass. —late summer, 1929.

LOWRY and AIKEN hold the bottles from the last scene. They are drunk, happy, and have arms around one another.

LOWRY & AIKEN: *singing*
    My pa he can curse, my ma she can cry,
    They'll all forgive me in the sweet bye-and-bye.
    I come from heaven, and to heaven I'll go,
    But it's what's in between I'm awanting to know.

LOWRY:
    Avast the chorus!

AIKEN:
    I don't know the bloody chorus!

LOWRY:
    To hell with it then.

        They sit, and LOWRY puts an oyster shell he is holding
        up to his ear.

AIKEN:
    What are you doing with those shells?

LOWRY: *holding a shell to his ear*
    Listening to the sound of the sea.

AIKEN:
    Malc, you jerk, they're oyster shells! You can't hear the
    sea in oyster shells!

LOWRY: *holding a shell to AIKEN's ear*
    Sure you can. It's a question of point of view. Here.
    Listen.

AIKEN:
    Come on...!

LOWRY:
    Shhhhh.

AIKEN: *listening to the shell*
    What am I supposed to hear?

LOWRY: *whispering*
    The oyster's dream of the sea.

AIKEN: *chuckling and dropping shell*
    "I too have heard the sea sounds in strange
    waters."   *Beat.*   Remember that? You wrote that.
    Your first letter to me.

LOWRY:

Second actually. Not counting all the self-conscious attempts I tore up. But here's to the first, and the courage I somehow found to beg you to take me on as...the sorcerer's apprentice.

AIKEN: *after a pause*
The summer's nearly over.

LOWRY:

I thought if we both ignored it, it might just keep sailing on.

AIKEN:
What'll you do now?

LOWRY:

Out of my hands, old boy. Keep my promise to my father. Return to merry England...prepare for Cambridge.

AIKEN:
Maybe it won't be all that bad.

LOWRY:

Come on, Conrad. You detest that world as much as I do. Creeky old dons with the souls of twice-boiled haddock; overfleshed matrons tottering about the greensward with orange squashes and Bath buns in their liver spotted paws..."I say, what a ripping idea, papaw."   *Beat.*   And I'm sure that's the uplifting side.

AIKEN: *amused*
I wish I could disagree.   *Pause.*   You'll finish the novel, I hope.

LOWRY:

In time. Thanks to you and your bleeding ebb and flow. *Beat.* It'll take a while. I've absorbed so much of you...I don't know where I begin any more. I feel like a little, not-so-accomplished Aiken.

AIKEN:

Don't underrate yourself, Malc. You absorb so fast it frightens me. Really.

LOWRY: *after a pause*

And what happens to the big Aiken now?

AIKEN:

My divorce comes through...I'll marry Jerry...provided she's still speaking to me after this summer.... Live off some free-lance for a while. The plot of a third-rate novel, eh?

LOWRY:

You'll never fall into that, Conrad. Whatever you do, it won't be third-rate.

AIKEN:

Don't give me false hopes, child. I'm going to serve you a warning. Now. Culture...and remember this...

LOWRY:

Yes, master.

AIKEN:

LISTEN! DAMN YOU!! Culture is not passed on voluntarily from the old to the young. The young take it. Take it, Malc. It's not a question of gifts. It's a question of theft. Maybe even...a form of destruction.

LOWRY:

Is that how you got it? Theft?

AIKEN:

Even now, when I'm shaving, I find myself trying to look like my father.

LOWRY:

I have to confess...these days when I'm shaving...

AIKEN:

You shave?!

LOWRY:

...these days when I'm shaving, I try to look like you.

AIKEN:

There you go. Transmission of values. Oh dear! I have such a hard time trying to look like my father. I really do.

LOWRY:

Why?

AIKEN:

I look like my mother.

LOWRY:

Poor woman!

AIKEN:

Seriously. Don't laugh. Her only outstanding quality was her pigs. She drew the most fantastic pigs. Fat and smiling with little watch-spring tails. They were the essence of piggyness.   *Beat.*   I can't draw a pig to save my life.

LOWRY:

Here's to your pigs...and an unforgettable summer.

AIKEN:

God. Yes. Malc, you've given me something. Hope, maybe. I don't know. It's not just the crass flattery of having a disciple. Much more. For a while there I was beginning to feel that the best was over.

LOWRY:

Just beginning, Conrad.

AIKEN:

Damn right. The bare beginnings. Damn bloody right.

LOWRY:

You know, I was beginning to feel a bit at the end of things too.

AIKEN:

For Chrissake! You're nineteen, you little bugger!

LOWRY:

And a bit. But keep in mind, old bird, I've fulfilled all my early dreams...shipped out on a freighter, knocked about the ports of the world: Kuwait, Kowloon, Canton...places people spend a lifetime simply hoping to see.

AIKEN:

You're still a child, you idiot!

LOWRY: *pulling up trouser leg and pointing*
See that scar...side of the kneecap. That's a bullet wound...

AIKEN:

That's a gravel rash!

LOWRY:

...I got winged during a Boxer riot in Hong Kong.

AIKEN:

> The last time I heard that story, you lying little scut, it was Canton.

LOWRY:

> The trauma of an experience like that. It mutes the mind.

AIKEN:

> You said Canton. Very clearly.

LOWRY:

> I was drunk...probably pissed.

AIKEN:

> Canton. You said Canton.

LOWRY:

> Well, damn it, Conrad! You know these Chinese towns.

AIKEN:

> They all look alike, I suppose! See that scar? In the shape of a cross?

LOWRY:

> You cut yourself praying.

AIKEN:

> I got that fighting a romantic young liar who is under the raving delusion that he's going to be the greatest novelist since Dostoi-bloody-evsky!

LOWRY:

> Say you don't mean that.

AIKEN:

> Come here, boy. Give me one of those bear hugs of yours. Godalmighty Malc, I'm going to miss you. I do believe in you. Maybe that's the problem. I believe in you too much.

Blackout.

Musical Bridge: Noel Coward singing "Just Around the Corner."

Scene Five

A restaurant, London, England—1930.

ARTHUR O. LOWRY sits at a table waiting. He is a dour, serious man. An Edwardian entrepreneur leaning on an expensive cane. AIKEN comes in and stands over the table.

AIKEN:
Excuse me, Mr. Lowry?

ARTHUR:
Yes?

AIKEN:
Conrad Aiken.   *Beat.*   I'm sorry I've kept you waiting.

ARTHUR:
Your jacket. American cut. I notice these things.

AIKEN:
Of course. It's your business, isn't it?

ARTHUR:
Indirectly, Mr. Aiken. I'm on the Board of the Liverpool Cotton Exchange. We don't deal in finished products. We do, however, meet a lot of Americans.

AIKEN:
Shall we order a drink or something?

ARTHUR:
Thank you, no. It's not one of my vices, I confess. Not a case, I regret, of like father, like son.

AIKEN:
Tea...or perhaps a coffee?

ARTHUR:
I was about to welcome you to England, but my son tells me you've lived here before.

AIKEN:
Often. I like to think of England as my mother, the United States, my father.

ARTHUR:
I see, yes. Very nice for you. Very nice.   *Beat.*
Forgive my bluntness, Mr. Aiken...it happens to be one of MY vices...would you mind if I came directly to the point?

AIKEN:
If you wish.

ARTHUR:
You had a chance to observe Malcolm last year...I know so very little about these things. In your opinion, is my son an alcoholic?

AIKEN: *thrown*
Ah...Mr. Lowry...I...I hardly expected.... Alcoholism is a very...loaded word.

ARTHUR:
I see I've baffled you with the question. Very well, let me be more precise. Has he degenerated to the point that he is physically or mentally dependent on alcohol? Is that straightforward enough, Mr. Aiken?

AIKEN:

It's not a question of being straightforward. Nor, sir, in Malcolm's case, is it a question of alcohol. There are other considerations.

ARTHUR:

For example. I wish to understand.

AIKEN:

Mr. Lowry...I'm really not qualified to discuss this question.

ARTHUR:

You are making this very difficult for me.

AIKEN:

Malcolm told me you had something to discuss with me. If this is it, Mr. Lowry, I'm afraid you've wasted a trip to London. I'm sorry.

ARTHUR:

Mr. Aiken...last year, at Malcolm's urging, I employed you, sight unseen...at quite a respectable salary, I'm sure you'll agree...to tutor my son. Is it asking too much for a straightforward report of his behaviour during your term of employment?

AIKEN: *rising to anger*

In the first place, sir...it was less a case of you employing me, as you choose to put it, than my accepting Malcolm as my student and my guest. An acceptance, I remind you, based on my assessment of his promise as a writer. A writer, Mr. Lowry. Which brings me to my second point....

ARTHUR:

Please. Understand what I'm saying...

39

AIKEN:

Understand! What I don't understand is why the hell your first question to me is not: Does my son have the makings of a good writer? No! You want an analysis of his behaviour patterns!

ARTHUR:

Perhaps I haven't made myself very clear...

AIKEN: *standing*

To the contrary.   *Beat.*   I'm a writer with more than a modicum of credibility. That's what I am. Now I'll tell you what I'm not, Mr. Lowry. I'm not a teacher for hire. And worse, I'm not a psychoanalyst. And if it's possible to get even worse than that, I'm certainly not your son's keeper!   *Beat.*   Excuse me, I see no value in continuing this conversation.

ARTHUR: *rising*

Please...I was overzealous...rude...Mr. Aiken, would you please sit down again?   *Beat.*   Please.

AIKEN hesitates, studies him, shrugs and returns and sits.

Thank you.   *Pause.*   May I ask...do you have any children?

AIKEN:

Three. By my first marriage.

ARTHUR:

A broken home. Most unfortunate. For the children, I mean.

AIKEN:

One doesn't plan these things, Mr. Lowry. They happen anyway.

ARTHUR:
Yes, of course.   *Beat.*   Malcolm...is my youngest.
I have three other boys...they're hardly boys now.
Having children too, you'll understand a father's...

AIKEN: *interrupting*
Your son is one of the most brilliant and gifted young
men I've ever met. Believe me.

ARTHUR:
Ah! Brilliant. Gifted.

AIKEN:
I would go so far as to say, perhaps even a potential
genius.

ARTHUR:
It's most gratifying to hear that. I must confess I
associate the idea of genius more with...music, perhaps.
Composing or playing an instrument, rather than novel
writing. Excuse me, you know more about these things
than I. My son thinks very highly of you. It almost
amounts to worship.   *Beat.*   Perhaps I'm a
little...envious of that. His mother and I...have done
everything possible. The best schools. He wanted to go
to sea, and I arranged a job for him on one of our
freighters. Did he tell you that?   *Beat.*   When he
wanted to study with you, I assisted him...and you
know, of course, that I provide him with a regular
allowance through my lawyers here in London. I know
he resents that...having to come in and pick it up, but
it's the only way I have of assuring myself that he's still
alive. And from what the lawyers tell me...Good Lord!
Is it' brilliant to be drunk and irresponsible? To swill
down alcohol day and night and reel about the streets?
Is this brilliance?!

AIKEN:
Mr. Lowry...

ARTHUR:

If he has all these gifts you claim...isn't this a shameful waste?

AIKEN:

For a young man his age...yes, he drinks far too much. But he works also. For long hours, and with terrifying determination. He has a spark of genius. That in itself is an abnormal condition...I should say, a supernormal condition. With this kind of genius, there comes a curse...the curse of NOT being normal. Can you understand that?

ARTHUR:

And this forgives everything, does it? Mr. Aiken...you speak of genius and curses and abnormality. I speak of my son. Can you understand THAT?

AIKEN looks at him, and the two exchange a long stare. Finally ARTHUR turns his head away.

Can you help him?   *Beat.*   Will you help him?

AIKEN:

As a writer, for a while. Possibly.

ARTHUR:

I believe I mean, as a man, Mr. Aiken.

AIKEN looks at him, trying to discern something. Anything.

AIKEN: *shaking his head*
I couldn't promise that.

ARTHUR:

Now that I've talked to you... *Pause.* Would you be willing to serve as...I suppose guardian is the most suitable word...dispense Malcolm's allowance...help him as best you can? I will ask no promises, and of course I will, in return, provide you with a monthly retainer. A sum of mutual agreement.

AIKEN:

Is this your idea, or Malcolm's?

ARTHUR:

Let's simply say, he put the idea into my head. If you agree, we could go over to the lawyer's now and set out the contract.

AIKEN: *absently*

In loco parentis.

ARTHUR:

I believe that's the legal term, yes. I find Latin makes things sound rather threatening, don't you?

AIKEN:

Perhaps. Yes. *Beat.* Terribly threatening.

Blackout.

Musical Bridge: Opening bars of "Dancing in the Dark."

Scene Six

Parlour, AIKEN's house, Rye, Sussex—1931.

As the lights come up, CLARISSA LORENZ AIKEN sites impatiently waiting, and then pacing.

AIKEN and LOWRY enter. Both are a little drunk, and AIKEN is wearing a raincoat that is splattered with mud. As they enter, AIKEN is in the midst of an intense, though rambling discussion with with LOWRY.

AIKEN:

That so-called poet, Tom Eliot, and all those damn dry dumb disquisitions on metaphysics...a broken man crawling towards Aristotle. I'm a better poet then he is, and he bloody well knows it. Is it my fault the bastard's in vogue, for God's sake?

CLARISSA:
Conrad?

AIKEN:
Ah! Jerry.

CLARISSA:
What happened?

AIKEN:

Malc and I were having a discussion here and we could use another opinion.

CLARISSA:
You're covered in mud!

AIKEN:
I know what it is.   *Beat.*   Now, if you...

CLARISSA:
Will you please tell me what's happened!

AIKEN:
I fell in the mud, Jerry. Now can I ask my question?

CLARISSA:
Malcolm, you tell me.

LOWRY:
He fell in the mud, Clarissa.

AIKEN:
Well, I'm glad we're all agreed on that. Now, you can settle an argument for us...

CLARISSA:
I've had dinner in the oven for five hours! You could at least have called. We do have a phone, you know!

LOWRY: *sheepishly*
I'm afraid it's my fault, Clarissa. I'm awfully sorry.

CLARISSA:
Stay out of this, Malcolm. I'm tired of you taking the blame for his thoughtlessness.

AIKEN:
Thanks anyway, old horse.

CLARISSA:
Stop this buddy-buddy shit! Bit of a drink, bit of a laugh, and you think everything's solved!   *Beat.*
Every time I call up the pubs in the area to ask if you're there...The moment I say I'm your wife, I'm immediately told that you haven't been in all evening. That's a little suspicious, isn't it?

AIKEN:
You mean to tell me you've been sitting here all evening with the phone book checking the pubs?

CLARISSA:
I don't need the damn phone book! I know the numbers by heart now!

LOWRY:

Oh Lord, I feel terrible about this. I'm causing problems, I think.

AIKEN:

Jerry, don't get started...

LOWRY:

But it's true. These late nights happen every time I come down to stay with you, don't they?

CLARISSA:

No, Malcolm. Not just when you visit. Is it, Conrad? *Beat.* Is it?

AIKEN:

Jerry, please.

CLARISSA:

I never get to see you any more. When you're at home, you're always locked away in your room writing. What the hell am I doing here? Let me know when you're available, Conrad...and I'll make an appointment.

> *She exits, and there is a long uncomfortable pause in the room.*

AIKEN:

Cabin fever, I think it's called. Clarissa doesn't know too many people here, and those she does are more than a shade critical of my way of life, I'm afraid. Can't blame her, I suppose.

LOWRY:

They're jealous, old bird. You're having too much fun.

AIKEN:

Malc, how much do you know about sex?

LOWRY:
    Sex?

AIKEN:
    S...E...X, sex. That damnable, divine instinct.
    Ostensibly provided to ensure the perpetuation of the
    species. And if I'm anything to go by, a species
    apparently terrified by the thought of annihilation.
    Beat.   I practise perpetuation in criminal amounts.

LOWRY:
    I'm sorry, I don't follow you.

AIKEN: *ignoring him*
    The sex urge, passion, lust...whatever.... It's like this
    great, destructive river ripping its way over the land,
    devouring. And in all the world, there is only one thing
    that can stop it. One thing that can freeze it like a
    winter stream.

LOWRY:
    What's that?

AIKEN:
    A bloody headache.   *Beat.*   Isn't that
    hilarious?   *Beat.*   Speaking of which, I have to
    work on tomorrow's.   *He drinks.*   You're a virgin,
    aren't you?

LOWRY:
    I wouldn't say that.

AIKEN:
    Don't give me this bullshit about making it with a
    prostitute in Canton or wherever. Keep that for your
    novel.   *Beat.*   Square with me, Malcolm. You're a
    twenty-four year old virgin, aren't you?

LOWRY:
    NO!   *Pause.*   I'm twenty-three.

AIKEN:

Is it a problem for you?

LOWRY:

What?

AIKEN:

You heard me. Is it a problem?

LOWRY: *getting angry*

NO!

AIKEN:

You have your ways of handling it, then?

LOWRY:

What are you talking about?

AIKEN:

You know damn well. Don't be cute.

LOWRY:

Okay, I DON'T have my ways of handling it, as you put it.

AIKEN: *scoring a point*

Then you have no sex drive, I take it.

LOWRY:

Of course I do.

AIKEN:

Look, either you've got no sex drive, or you have your ways of handling it. Take your choice. It's one or the other.

LOWRY:

Stop it, Conrad! I don't know what you're getting at, but if you want to fight, go fight with your wife.

AIKEN:
Yes, I know. You lift weights. You'll bounce me off the walls, won't you?

LOWRY:
Conrad?

AIKEN:
Don't worry. I know you can do it. Got the scars to prove it. *Beat.* Let history record, however, that I did win the toilet seat, Lowry.

LOWRY:
What's wrong with you tonight? What's eating you?

AIKEN:
How the hell would you know? You're a virgin who can't make up his mind if he's got a sex drive or not.

LOWRY:
For God's sake! I don't understand you tonight!

AIKEN:
Just wait. You will. *Beat.* I have another question, and I want a straight answer to this one. I'm entrusted with your welfare by a man whose ability to judge character is rivalled only by Caesar's. But this Brutus here wants to know one thing. Why the hell are you boozing yourself to death?

AIKEN goes to sit down, but misses the chair and collapses onto the floor. LOWRY goes over and helps him to his feet and into the chair.

LOWRY:
I might ask you the same thing.

AIKEN:
You're a young man...with promise. Incredible promise.

LOWRY:
That's why you drink so heavily?

AIKEN:
Don't twist my words, Malc! I'm talking about you.

LOWRY:
Conrad, I'll never be as good as you. I'm your apprentice, heir...I always will be.

AIKEN:
God! You're naive! You really are.

LOWRY:
About sex, perhaps. But not about you.

AIKEN: *handing him the bottle*
Here, have another drink. It might accelerate the process.   *Beat.*   Children, heirs...I ever tell you about them?

LOWRY:
What about them?

AIKEN:
It all begins with a little muffled thump on the tympanum of the womb, right? Boomp...boomp. Like that. Doesn't sound dangerous at all...soft and kind of warm. Then they slide into the light. Bang! There they are.   *Beat.*   Bang! Now I...I maintain a delusion of superiority with pride. A father's pride at their making...as I gaze down on the little heads oiled with mucous...anointed by ME. But HELL! There they are...destined to grow powerful as I languish and weaken. Destined to usurp! Destined to triumph where I fail!   *growing faint*   Me...good as dead and buried...and all I have to hold to is a pathetic shred of pride. Pride. Is it any wonder it's the first sin...reason for the Fall?

LOWRY:

A case of the seeds of destruction in the creation, I believe.

AIKEN:

It's so...tangible...so clear to me. God! I could shriek it from the rooftops.

LOWRY: *nodding*
Yes.

AIKEN:

Don't say yes! Say YES!! *Beat.* What the hell do you know about it? *Beat.* VIRGIN!

LOWRY:

Bugger off, Conrad!

AIKEN:

The story of history right there. Man eats the apple, God says: bugger off! One generation goes to war, topples empires, and the next one says: bugger off! All of bloody human history echoes with the sounds of little feet, buggering off!!

LOWRY: *laughing*
Bugger off!

AIKEN:

Horrifying, isn't it? Oh, Malc! Let's change it. For once in the pathetic history of this pathetic world, let's smash the goddamn order of things! What do you say?
Beat. I mean, I'm really not enjoying this role of the aging would-be Cassanova...navigating through life with an erection forward, and a flapping shirt-tail out the back. It's not...dignified, for a start. *Beat.* Yes, that's what's bothering Jerry. If you weren't such an innocent you would have guessed by now. At the moment, thank God, she just suspects. *Beat.* But all this activity! It's not helping! It's not working! OH HELL! Let's break the order of things!!

LOWRY:
"Art requires the ultimate sacrifice."

AIKEN:
What?!

LOWRY:
"Art requires the ultimate sacrifice." Don't you know your own words when you hear them?

AIKEN:
What the hell are you talking about? What's art got to do with it?

LOWRY:
I think I was talking about...life.

> *AIKEN laughs, stands and exits calling out CLARISSA'S name seductively.*

> *Blackout.*

Scene Seven

Venereal Disease Museum, Liverpool, England—1930.

ARTHUR O. LOWRY stands in the Venereal Disease Museum in Liverpool. The drop screens now display a gallery of horrors: malformed foetuses of miscarried embryos in large bottles of alcohol.

LOWRY enters.

LOWRY: *gazing about in horror*
Father, why did you bring me here?

ARTHUR:
You know this place?

LOWRY:
My brothers dragged me here when I was little. Their
idea of a joke.

ARTHUR:
Venereal disease is not a joke, Malcolm.

LOWRY:
I was terrified.   *Beat.*   Please, can we go?

ARTHUR:
When I first saw this Museum, I could not believe the
world contained such things. I still find it...difficult to
accept. I'm not an untravelled man, as you know, but
this...this, truly shocked me. Born, of man, and
spawned in the gutters of depravity. And yet, we must
remind ourselves, constantly Malcolm, that these are not
products of the imagination. They are the real
corruptions of mortal flesh. Mortal flesh, Malcolm, of
which we are all made. Can you see that?

LOWRY: *closing his eyes*
Father, why did you bring me here?

ARTHUR:
Look about you, Malcolm. LOOK! Before it's too late,
boy! This is where your life is leading, Malcolm. Step
out of the pure light of God's blessing, step out of the
goodness, the rightness of this world, and this is where
you will be cast. This...HELL! I am ordering
you...   *Beat.*   Dear God! I am begging you!
Come back while you still may. I don't want this world
for you, my son.

LOWRY:
Those are foetuses, aren't they? Unborn children.

ARTHUR:
Miscarried through syphilis.

LOWRY:
Bottled in jars of alcohol for eternity.

ARTHUR:
Yes. One of the rare cases, I'm told, where alcohol
serves as a preservative.

LOWRY:
Look at the faces. I think I envy them. They seem so at
peace.

ARTHUR:
Sweet Heaven! How can you speak of peace in a place
like this? I don't understand you, boy. This morbidity.
This ugliness. If you want to write, write about the
beauty of life. Out there.

LOWRY:
If there's truly beauty in the world, Father, it must be
here too.

ARTHUR: *noticing LOWRY's hands*
Why, you're shaking.

LOWRY:
You know the really ironic thing about this place,
Father?

> *LOWRY's shakes stubbornly persist. He reaches in his
> jacket and pulls out a fifth of gin. He unscrews the top
> and offers his father a swig, without thinking.*

...the really very ironic thing about it? It's the name of
the street it's on. That ever occur to you?

LOWRY becomes conscious of his father staring in horror at the proffered fifth. LOWRY reacts to what he is doing, and quickly shoves it back in his pocket.

ARTHUR:
I can do no more. You're lost to me, Malcolm.
Beat. Goodbye, I'll leave you to this. It's what you obviously desire.

ARTHUR LOWRY exits, head bent. LOWRY watches him leaving, confused. He reaches into his back pocket, takes a pull on the fifth, and calls after his father.

LOWRY:
It's called Paradise Street, Father. Paradise Street. Yes, Paradise Street.

Blackout.

Musical Bridge: Tarrega's "Recuerdos de la Alahambra Tango."

Scene Eight

Patio, Pension Carmona, Grenada, Spain—1933.

The screens provide a feeling of lightness and colour, a sense of the festive and exotic.

AIKEN walks on with ED BURRA. BURRA has a sharp thin face and a cynical attitude to match. He carries a sketch pad and pencil with him.

BURRA:

It was grotesque, Conrad. Utterly grotesque.

AIKEN:

I disagree. He fought well and made an extremely clean kill.

BURRA:

I thought bullfighters were supposed to be tall, good-looking Conquistador types. Did you see that man? Face like a demented ferret. A most unpleasant little creature. Frankly, I was pulling for the bull. It was infinitely better looking.

AIKEN:

And supposing, just supposing, for the sake of argument, the bullfighter looked like Rudolph Valentino.

BURRA:

I would've instantly switched my loyalties, of course. I'm a painter, chum. A visual person. Unattractive things depress the hell out of me. *Beat.* Speaking of unattractive things, that piss-tank Lowry and his vamp seemed to enjoy the whole gory spectacle.

AIKEN:

Jan is not a vamp.

BURRA:

Oh indeed.

AIKEN:

She's simply a very sociable woman.

BURRA:

Oh come on, Conrad. If anyone took the time to record her conquests, it would look like the casualty list of the Titanic!

AIKEN:
So, she's not a virgin.

BURRA:
Since the day you introduced the two of them, they've been going at it like demented rabbits.

AIKEN:
They're enjoying themselves, that's all.

BURRA:
Frankly, I'm amazed we got them to the corrida at all. It's at least a mile from the nearest bed.

AIKEN:
Drop it, okay, Ed?

BURRA:
All right, old friend. No offence. I'm a great believer in coincidence. I only hope Clarissa shares that with me.

AIKEN:
What are you talking about?

BURRA:
Conrad, it's painfully obvious that you know this Gabriel woman quite well, and I seriously doubt she indulges in platonic encounters. It's amazing that she just happened to turn up in Grenada at the same time as we did.

AIKEN:
Ed, can you paint with your feet?

BURRA:
I sincerely doubt it.

AIKEN:
I hear another comment like that coming out of your mouth, you better start learning.

BURRA:

My God! Bullfights really bring the Al Capone out in you, don't they?

CLARISSA enters.

CLARISSA:

I think it's going to be a beautiful evening.

BURRA:

Ah, Clarissa, Conrad here was just explaining the finer points of a matador's cape work to me. He's convinced me it's an art.

AIKEN:

It is an art.

CLARISSA:

I've never seen anything so ugly. I'd rather not hear about it, thank you. I ran into Malcolm and Jan. He said they'd be down to join us shortly.

BURRA:

Let me guess. They were headed for the bedroom.

CLARISSA:

They're always headed for the bedroom.

AIKEN:

Jesus!

CLARISSA:

Don't be such a stick in the mud, dear. They're in love.

BURRA: *to CLARISSA*

I have the room next to them, Clarissa pet. That Gabriel woman trumpets her orgasms like a Wagnerian heroine. Do you have any idea what it's like being subjected to a whole night of the Ring Cycle?

CLARISSA: *enjoying this immensely*
Is she at least on key?

AIKEN:
Look, you don't want to talk about bullfighting. I don't
want to talk about opera.

CLARISSA: *to CONRAD*
You're a little testy, today.

AIKEN:
I'm not testy, Jerry.

CLARISSA:
You just seemed a little testy.

BURRA:
She has a point, Conrad. I was looking for the right
word. Testy seems appropriate.

AIKEN:
I...am...not...testy! Could a testy man smile with such
gay abandon?

      AIKEN flashes a forced lurid grin.

CLARISSA:
I think it's wonderful to see Malcolm finally taking an
interest in a woman. It's what you wanted for him,
Conrad.

AIKEN:
I advised him to lose his virginity, Jerry. Not beat it to
bloody death!

CLARISSA:
Look at the change in him. He's almost normal.

BURRA:
Let's not push it, pet. He's just a little less repulsive.

59

AIKEN:

Repulsive! It's revolting! When he's not with her, he's primping and preening in front of the mirror. Looks like a mesmerized owl in a terminal trauma! It's utterly revolting!

CLARISSA:

It's a change for the better.

AIKEN:

At least he was Malcolm before.

CLARISSA:

Sure it was Malcolm. Swilling down booze, incoherent, insulting our friends when he wasn't throwing up in their laps. Now that he's finally found someone else to lean on, this might be the time to drop the contract with his father.

AIKEN:

I think you're right.

CLARISSA:

Then perhaps we can spend more time together.

AIKEN:

On top of everything else, I don't think this Gabriel woman is quite what the doctor ordered.

CLARISSA:

A bit...worldly, perhaps. But as I recall, the doctor didn't order her. You introduced her to Malcolm.

AIKEN:

It was a mistake, okay?

CLARISSA:

At the risk of sounding the jealous wife...how did you happen to know her?

BURRA:
Actually, Clarissa, I introduced them. Years ago, wasn't it? A cockfight in Marseille, as I recall. Jan loves cockfights.

AIKEN glares at BURRA.

AIKEN:
Anybody fancy some Sangria?

BURRA:
Oh, that bloody awful red haemorrhaging stuff. Love some. *Beat.* Conrad? While you're in there, would you ask that Iberian half-wit of a bartender what the hell all this gunfire is about every night? Are they knocking off peasants a la Goya or what?

AIKEN:
Stray cats. The police collect them for fodder.

BURRA:
That's it! I'm going vegetarian. You just accounted for that odd-tasting lamb I had last night!

AIKEN exits.

He's a touch of the laughing Cavalier today.

CLARISSA:
This whole thing with Malcolm isn't helping, Ed. He wants to drop the contract with Malcolm's father. But it's hard for him.

BURRA:
Hard for him! He's been led up the garden path. God knows how! That kid's no budding genius. I've seen a thousand like him. Outcasts of the literary left. They wear the cloak of tortured brilliance and booze themselves into oblivion because it's a damn sight easier

61

to drink than to write. Creepy little pseudo-Rimbauds popping up in the turds of bygone romantics. I don't know how Conrad ever bought that load of shit, anyway.

CLARISSA:
There's something between the two of them. Conrad says it's a spiritual union, but there's more.

BURRA:
Good Lord! You're not suggesting...? Clarissa, I've known him for years. He's an Olympic heterosexual. I couldn't begin to count...   *Pause.*   I mean, in his youth, of course.

CLARISSA: *in despair*
Oh Christ!

BURRA:
Take it easy, pet.

CLARISSA:
Damn it! What's going on? Where am I in all of this? Where's Conrad? Why...?!   *breaking*   Please, Ed. Please. What's happening here? I think I'm losing him and I don't know why.

BURRA:
Clarissa....

> *Before BURRA can finish, LOWRY and JAN GABRIEL walk on stage arm in arm. JAN is a tall attractive woman in her early 20s, with a sultry air about her. She is vogue fashion to the teeth. LOWRY is obviously head over heels in love with her.*

JAN:
Hi everybody. Mind if we join you?

BURRA:
>I find the suggestion barely tolerable, but go ahead.

LOWRY:
>What a wonderful bullfight! There's a physical poetry about it.

BURRA:
>Which part did you like best, Jan? The lance in the neck, or the sword through the heart?

JAN:
>I loved all of it. Malcolm sees it as a sort of ritual killing. Very primitive and archetypal.

BURRA:
>That doesn't surprise me.

LOWRY:
>You have to isolate the images. Blood congealing in the hot sand. The flash of cold metal over dark driving muscle.

BURRA:
>Oh dear! I feel a primitive and archetypal shiver running up my back!

>>*AIKEN comes in carrying a jug of sangria and a handful of glasses.*

LOWRY:
>Conrad? Do you know Jan's read all of your books?

AIKEN: *to JAN*
>I always suspected masochism was one of your traits.

JAN:
>Not really. I'm simply in the habit of finishing anything I start.

BURRA:
> Regardless of race, colour or creed, I should imagine.

CLARISSA:
> You have any favourites, Jan?

JAN:
> I find it difficult to be critical of my favourite writers.
> Malcolm's been reading me bits of his novel. I think it's
> wonderful.   *suggestively*   He's learned a lot from
> you, I suspect, Conrad.

CLARISSA:
> Conrad hates teaching. It's really quite remarkable, I
> think.

BURRA:
> Olé!!

JAN:
> Malcolm's a very good reader. Dramatic.

CLARISSA:
> I always enjoyed it when Conrad would read to me. At
> night. In bed.

JAN:
> I know what you mean.

CLARISSA:
> Really?

JAN:
> Malcolm reads to me in bed, too.

BURRA:
> He must be hoarse by now.

> *BURRA has begun doing a sketch of LOWRY.*

CLARISSA:
>It's the real source of all fiction, don't you think, Jan? Tales in bed?

JAN:
>Waking dreams.

LOWRY:
>Why that's lovely, Jan.

BURRA:
>I wish you two bastards could read to me some time. I could use the sleep. Lowry? How's the novel coming?

LOWRY:
>It's not finished yet.

BURRA:
>What are you working for? The record gestation period for a creative work?

>>*BURRA has finished the sketch of LOWRY. He passes it to CLARISSA.*

CLARISSA: *amused*
>Oh really, Ed! That's quite unfair.

>>*Through the following, the sketch goes into AIKEN's hands.*

LOWRY:
>Jan, can't you stay a few more days. Please.

JAN:
>I'm sorry, Malcolm. I'm expected in Paris. I've no choice.

AIKEN: *looking at sketch; to BURRA*
>You have a talent. Perverse. But a talent.

CLARISSA:
Oh you're leaving us already, Jan? What a shame.

JAN:
I'm afraid so.

> *LOWRY moves to the group around the table. There is an uncomfortable silence as LOWRY looks at the sketch.*

Oh Malcolm, this is the best damn holiday I've ever had. I'm going to miss you all so very much.   *trying to brighten the mood*   I'd like to propose a toast...

> *LOWRY tears up the sketch into small pieces and throws it at BURRA.*

BURRA:
It was just in fun, Lowry...just in fun.

> *LOWRY storms out. JAN follows. BURRA finishes his sangria as CLARISSA exits with the jug of sangria. After a pause AIKEN follows her. BURRA collects the torn pieces of his sketch and he, too, exits.*

> *Lights fade down.*

> *The repeated sounds of gunshots.*

Scene Nine

Same—later that evening.

The stage is in semi-darkness, with only faint keys forming pools of light. LOWRY sits morose, drinking.

AIKEN comes on-stage and halts, looking about and waiting for his eyes to become accustomed to the dark.

AIKEN: *calling softly*
Malcolm? You out here? Malcolm?

LOWRY: *after a pause*
Yes?

AIKEN:
Say something.   *Pause.*   I was trying to do some writing...but it's too stuffy inside. And those damn gunshots.

LOWRY: *absently*
Oh. Yes. Bit of a nuisance, aren't they? Cats, you said. Stray animals.

AIKEN:
No, it's the police doing the shooting. I don't think the cats have guns.

LOWRY:
You know what I mean.

AIKEN:
Come on, Malc. I could use a smile tonight.

LOWRY:
Have a drink instead.   *Beat.*   I've never felt this way before. About anybody.

AIKEN:
That's the problem, is it?

LOWRY:
I'm in love with her, old boy. Sad condition, eh?

67

AIKEN:
A holiday infatuation. Like a sunburn, it'll fade in time.

LOWRY:
Don't make fun of me, Conrad. I'm bloody serious.

AIKEN:
So am I. You'll get over it. Jan does that to men, you know.

LOWRY:
I don't intend getting over it, as you put it. I'm going to marry her.

AIKEN: *amused*
Indeed. What's she have to say about that?

LOWRY:
It's what I have to say.

AIKEN:
Did you ask her?

LOWRY:
We talked about it. Yes.

AIKEN:
She didn't agree, did she? *Beat.* All right, let me take a shot at it. "Malcolm, you're a sweet boy"...no. No. She'd say: "Malcolm, you're a terrific guy....It's been a fantastic couple of weeks, but I want to remember it just like this." *Beat.* How'd I do?

LOWRY:
Bugger off, Conrad. You're beginning to sound like that sneering friend of yours, Burra. Besides, it's none of your damn business.

AIKEN:
Malc, I don't want to see you making a mistake. Especially with her.

LOWRY:

You don't know her like I do. She's not like that.

AIKEN:

I know what she's like. She gets around, you know.

LOWRY:

Bugger the gossip. Suppose she'd listened to the stories
flying around about me, eh?

AIKEN:

It's not gossip, Malc.   *Pause.*   I've been there
before you, you know.

LOWRY:

YOU GODDAMN LIAR!

AIKEN:

Boy, you know me fairly well. Look at me.   *more*
insistent   LOOK AT ME!!   *Pause.*   She didn't
tell you, eh? If you don't believe what I'm saying, I'll
give you the intimate details. You'll know then, won't
you?

LOWRY:

I'LL KILL YOU!!

AIKEN:

I'm sorry I've got to hurt you like this, Malcolm. But
I've got to stop you.

LOWRY:

Knowing all this, why did you introduce me to her? No.
Correction. Shove me at her. Because that's exactly what
you did. Why?

AIKEN:

I thought it might help...get rid of that bothersome
virginity of yours. Help pull you together...

LOWRY:

No, Conrad. That doesn't wash. Now come on, let's get to the bottom of this...sordid little scheme of yours. You wanted her for yourself, didn't you?

AIKEN:

Don't be ridiculous!

LOWRY:

You wanted to spend the time here with her. Admit it. Of course you did, but you couldn't because of Clarissa, could you?   *Beat.*   But the next best thing was to pass her on to me. Share her...with the one person in the world who was a perfect extension of you. That way you wouldn't risk losing her entirely. Our little... conspiracy...would have guaranteed that for you, wouldn't it?

AIKEN:

You're drunk, Lowry.

LOWRY:

Perhaps. But astute, right Aiken? But I'm still missing something. A piece in the puzzle.

AIKEN:

This is absurd!

LOWRY:

I've got it! Yes! The fiction's not going according to your original plan, is it? After Jan left, you were going to admit to me that you'd been with her too. Yes? Yes. Then the two of us would nestle down in our grand, gilded club car, and in our grand, gilded conspiracy, wreathed in goddamn cigar smoke, sip our bloody brandies and swap descriptions about what a great lay she is. Yes? Yes. What a great fuck she is!   *Beat.* AND...AND, old bird...you knew my talent for verbal description. You should. You helped me bloody develop it. It's perfect. About as brilliant and sordid a voyeur's incestuous little scheme ever created.   *Beat*   Except for one thing. Go to hell, Aiken!!

AIKEN:
You ungrateful, drunken little bastard!

LOWRY:
Yes, I was wondering when you'd get to that. All right, let's give the screw another turn.

AIKEN:
I've heard all I want to hear from you.

LOWRY:
You sit there and listen to me, or so help me I'll knock you into place.   *Beat.*   Aiken, you've feared me from the first moment, haven't you? Feared me because I'm younger, stronger, and, until now, an uncompromised virgin.   *Beat.*   Right from the start you've protected yourself by absorbing me. Killing me. Making me the son, the drunk, the fool of the wise and understanding father. You even went so far as to engineer my fall from grace...my loss of virginity. Just to be sure I didn't have anything you didn't have. What was it you used to say to me back in Boston? Right. "Malcolm, the extension of the consciousness warrants the ultimate sacrifice." Finally, I understand it...DAD! You play the understanding father...while I get crucified. It's the one way you can fight the earthly order, isn't it?

AIKEN:
Can I leave now?

LOWRY:
No. You stay. Right where you've been all along. I'm going. It's my turn to kill you, old man. And I'm going to start by taking her away from you. I'm going after her. And if she'll have me, I'm going to marry

her.   *Beat.*   But that's just the first cut, Aiken.
I'm going to write as you never had the ability to write.
I'll bury you.   *Beat.*   I'm going to kill you,
Aiken. It's the natural order. I'm going to strip you to
the bone.

*LOWRY strides off the stage, as CLARISSA and
BURRA enter from the other side. They've obviously
overheard the last part of the conversation, and glance after
LOWRY with concern.*

CLARISSA:
Conrad! What's all the shouting about?

AIKEN:
Nothing, Jerry. Nothing.

CLARISSA:
I heard him threaten to kill you. What's going on?

AIKEN:
Have you been there long?

CLARISSA:
Ed and I were going down to see the fountains at night.

AIKEN:
Everything's fine. Malcolm's drunk and a little unhappy,
that's all.

BURRA:
Why don't you be done with that blasted dypsomaniac,
Conrad? He's making a misery for all of us.

AIKEN: *sadly*
I think it is done, Ed.

BURRA:
Good.

CLARISSA:
>Come on, dear. Join us. The man inside said the
>fountains are spectacular at night. All lit up like fairy
>castles. Didn't he, Ed?   *Beat.*   Please, Conrad.
>Please. For me?

AIKEN:
>Oh...no, I don't think so, Jerry. I'd like to sit here and
>think a bit, okay?

CLARISSA:
>All right, dear.   *Beat.*   Well, come along, Ed.

>*They exit as AIKEN stares away into the middle distance.*

>*AIKEN moves stage forward and gazes out over the
>audience.*

>*The NURSE enters, places a dressing gown around his
>shoulders, and he becomes an 85-year-old man again. The
>NURSE helps him off-stage.*

>*Lights fade.*

>*Final images remain on screens through intermission.*

>*Musical Bridge: Spanish theme as before.*

ACT TWO

Scene One

Rest home, Savannah, Georgia—1973.

*The screens, as in Act One, Scene One, show the interior
of the rest home. AIKEN sits in his bath chair with his
old robe on. He has a small folding table in front of him,
containing the remains of his lunch. He has a massive
napkin draped over his chest. He is, once again, an
85-year-old man. The NURSE calls to him from off-stage.
AIKEN is hiding from her, and giggles to himself over the
game he is playing with her.*

NURSE: *calling off-stage*
    Mr. Aiken? Mr. Aiken? Where are you? Mr. Aiken?

The NURSE enters, carrying a bowl.

Ah, there you are....Cook will be pleased! You've cleaned your plate for once. There you go.

She places the bowl on the tray in front of him. He stares at it, and then looks back at her quizzically.

It's dessert.

She is about to start out of the room when he speaks.

AIKEN:
It's Thursday!

NURSE:
Yes, it's Thursday. That's right.

AIKEN:
This is Thursday lunch!

NURSE:
It certainly is...

AIKEN:
Rice pudding!

NURSE: *looking in bowl*
Doesn't it look lovely.

AIKEN:
Rice pudding is Tuesday! Thursday is tapioca! This is Thursday!

NURSE:
Well, I guess cook decided to change it.

AIKEN:
I hate rice pudding. I put up with it on Tuesdays because we get it on Tuesdays. But I'm not going to eat it on Thursdays!   *Beat.*   I hate rice pudding. The sultanas get stuck in my teeth. They get stuck.

NURSE:
Well surely just this once...

AIKEN:
I won't eat rice pudding on Thursday! I want tapioca. I was expecting tapioca.

NURSE:
Very well. I'll talk to cook.

The NURSE starts out.

AIKEN:
Hey!

NURSE:
Yes?

AIKEN:
Don't put any of that spray shit on it. I don't want any spray shit.

NURSE:
I beg your pardon?

AIKEN looks at her then mimics holding a spray can of whipped cream. He makes a farting sound with his mouth to indicate what he's talking about. The NURSE grimaces, nods and is about to start away. She stops when he begins to speak again.

AIKEN:
My father was a doctor here in Savannah. Good one. Successful. We lived in a big white house.

NURSE:
Mr. Aiken?

AIKEN:
Probably not as big as I remember it being. But big.

NURSE:
Mr. Aiken?

AIKEN:
Well, one day...I was about twelve, I think...I was creeping downstairs after they had an argument, and I saw this strange thing...very strange thing.

LOWRY appears. He is drunk, unshaven and suffering a bad case of the shakes. As AIKEN is speaking, he becomes aware of the presence of LOWRY watching him. AIKEN turns, and panics for a moment.

Nurse!

LOWRY:
Go on.

AIKEN:
No! I don't want you! Leave me alone!

The NURSE, believing that AIKEN is talking to her, exits.

LOWRY: *prompting*
I saw this strange thing...

AIKEN:
I saw this strange thing...

LOWRY:
Go on.   *Beat.*   What's the matter?

AIKEN:
I'm trying to remember what I was trying to remember.

LOWRY:
Father.

AIKEN:

Why must you persecute me?!

LOWRY:

You were about twelve. You saw this strange thing.

AIKEN: *remembering*

My mother and father. They'd been arguing. I peeked
through these big old banisters. Saw them in the living
room. My father was sitting in her lap. Just like a
child...

LOWRY: *softly*

Like a child...

AIKEN:

With his arms around her neck. He was speaking to my
mother very softly.

LOWRY: *softly*

Like a child.

AIKEN:

"Maybe," he said, "we should have another child.
Maybe then you wouldn't go out so often. You wouldn't
be able to then." I was twelve and it was strange. Some
months...maybe weeks...later, I heard them arguing
again. Loud. I was playing in the front yard and I could
hear them all that way. I moved close to this huge old
oak we had...picked at the bark...touched it. When I
think of what happened that day...all I know is that's
what I see. The old oak. Rough and furrowed. The
argument went on for a long time, and then...I heard
my mother scream my father's name. Not loudly. Softly.
She actually screamed softly. There was a long
pause...and then I heard his voice. Counting. ONE.
TWO. THREE. Then I heard a gunshot. Filled the
house with silence. And after a while another shot. I
stayed, staring at the oak tree til my ears stopped
ringing with the silence...then I went inside. I don't
really remember seeing them. But I must have. My

mother shot through the head. My father...the gun was close to his face...he shoved it in his mouth, I guess, before.... Now all I can remember when I think of it...is a huge oak tree, like the very centre of the earth, its branches tangled high in a great vacant sky.

LOWRY:

I would have remembered the bullet holes, Conrad. There's the pain.

The NURSE enters. She comes over to AIKEN with a bowl of tapioca and hands it to him. He glances up at her, and then down at the bowl.

NURSE:

I think you ought to write a nice little note to cook. She prepared it especially for you.

The NURSE wheels AIKEN off as he slurps the tapioca ravenously, using his fingers and holding the bowl close, as if someone might snatch it from him.

Blackout.

Musical Bridge: A few bars of Duke Ellington's "Mood Indigo."

Scene Two

A basement flat, Bronx, New York—summer, 1935.

The screens provide the sense of a filthy, squalid basement flat in a Bronx tenement complex. LOWRY sits at a table writing with intense concentration, but with a case of the

79

shakes so severe, he is fighting to scribble every line. He looks a complete, unshaven wreck, and utters gasps of frustration at his spasmodic inability to hold a pencil.

AIKEN enters to one side.

AIKEN:
Malc?

LOWRY: *softly*
Come in.

AIKEN:
Malc?

LOWRY: *louder*
Come in!

AIKEN:
Malc!

LOWRY:
Oh for God's sake! Yes, what is it?!

AIKEN:
Malc?

LOWRY: *after a shocked pause*
Conrad!   *Beat.*   Is it really you, Conrad?

AIKEN:
Malc...how are you?

LOWRY:
Good Lord!

AIKEN:
Can I join you?

LOWRY:

Sorry, old boy. The shock...thought you might be one of the boarders here. It's a communal kitchen...you see, we all use it.

AIKEN:

This is quite...quaint.

LOWRY:

Nice touch of Yankee realism, I think.   *suddenly*
Be careful of the empty bottles.

AIKEN: *looking about*
There's enough of them.

LOWRY:

The others here...they're all unemployed. They sleep all day and play pinochle all night. This is the result.

AIKEN:

Quite the drinkers, eh?

LOWRY:

There should be a couple of full ones somewhere.

AIKEN:

Not for me, Malc. I just had breakfast.

LOWRY:

I can never tell the time of day down here. No windows. What the hell are you doing in New York, Conrad?

AIKEN:

Passing, as they say hereabouts.   *Beat.*   I had one devil of a time running you down.

LOWRY:

Yes...well...in hiding aren't I? Press has been driving me bats since *Ultramarine* came out. Fame is a terrible burden, old boy. Just terrible.

AIKEN: *amused*
Yes, I know what you mean.

LOWRY:
I sent you a copy of the novel. Did you get it?

AIKEN:
Indeed. Yes. My heartiest congratulations, Malc.

LOWRY:
Don't stand there squirming, I'm not going to ask you. I know already. Plagiarism in the following proportions. Forty percent Conrad Aiken, thirty percent Nordhall Grieg...remind me to tell you about him someday...and twenty-nine and a half percent Herman Melville. Right?

AIKEN:
What's the other half percent?

LOWRY:
The punctuation. THAT, at any rate, was my own. *Beat.* It's been duly noted, by the by, that you haven't disagreed.

AIKEN:
It's your first novel, Malc!

LOWRY:
Even the rare critic who had anything good to say about the book, made it sound like a bad mating of the Egyptian Book of the Dead, and Boys' Own Annual!

AIKEN:
Ah, bugger the critics!

LOWRY:
Ex-zactly! Bugger 'em. Bugger off, eh? *Beat.*
God I've missed you, old bird. I really
have. *Beat.* How's Clarissa?

AIKEN:
    Okay.   *Beat.*   How's Jan?

LOWRY:
    Marvellous. A-one. A-one.

AIKEN:
    That's good.

LOWRY:
    Yes, A-one.

    Pause.

    It's been...what? Two years, I guess?

AIKEN:
    Two. Almost to the day.

LOWRY: *awkwardly*
    Look...Conrad...I'm not like this all the time, old boy.
    Been on a real tear with some writing. I haven't washed
    or shaved...slept for that matter...for days, you see. I
    must look a bloody awful wreck.

AIKEN:
    You could stand a scrub.

LOWRY: *chuckling inanely*
    Bit of lime and soda, eh?   *Beat.*   Got a cigarette?
    Ran out a couple of days ago, and I'm dying for
    one.   *Aiken offers him a cigarette.*   See, this is just a
    temporary kind of thing here. Thanks. I...a...I actually
    prefer being down in a basement, with this ghastly
    heatwave putting the old parboil on New York. Seen the
    papers?

    *LOWRY searches his pants pockets as he talks, finds a
    package of matches and fumbles with them trying to light
    the cigarette. But his shakes create several abortive attempts.*

83

AIKEN watches the whole process with the same horror he has been uncomfortably regarding LOWRY with since his arrival.

AIKEN:
Want some help?

LOWRY:
Heat's already killed over a hundred people. Water shortages...God's creatures simply dessicating on the old pavement. *Beat.* Say...could you strike a match for me. I can't seem to curb this...problem.

AIKEN lights a cigarette and puts it into LOWRY'S mouth.

babbling It's lack of sleep. *Beat.* You know that's a lie, don't you? *Beat.* This room here is...it's infested with the most exotic insects. Not imagined. Real. Of great interest to science, I should think. But hell on someone trying to sleep.

AIKEN:
Given any thought to moving out of this dump?

LOWRY:
And lose all this atmosphere? You can't be serious. *Beat.* Hey...this is a special occasion. I'm being the most atrocious host. You must excuse me, old boy.

AIKEN:
Malc? Where's Jan?

LOWRY:
It's odd. I had a dream about you the other day. What was...? What was the little jingle your mother used to say to you when she put you to bed?

84

AIKEN:

Oh yes.   *Pause.*   One, two, three...and out goes
she.

LOWRY:

And she'd turn out the light.   *Beat.*   Yes. One,
two, three, and out goes she. I like that.

> *LOWRY finds a mickey and offers AIKEN a drink.*

AIKEN:

Not for me, Malc.

LOWRY:

You on the wagon these days?

AIKEN:

Dragging on the tailgate, you might say.

LOWRY:

Come on. Just this once. It's been years, after all.

AIKEN:

I guess. Sure, why not?

> *LOWRY accidentally fumbles the bottle as he is about to
> pass it to AIKEN.*

LOWRY:

Quite embarrassing, these shakes. I think just seeing
them makes them worse.   *Beat.*   Hope you're still
not angry about the wedding.

AIKEN:

Not being invited? At first. It's all past
now.   *Beat.*   Jan's not living with you, is she?

LOWRY:
No. *He wolfs down a drink.*   A little of the
necessary.   *Beat.*   We're going through one of
these newfangled self-expression separations. She's living
up on Columbus Circle. Up that way.

AIKEN:
I'm sorry. Truly.

LOWRY:
No need.   *Beat.*   I've got her number here
somewhere...I'm sure she'd love to hear from you.

> *AIKEN takes up the bottle.*

AIKEN:
Here's to seeing you again.

> *LOWRY snatches the bottle back before AIKEN can
> drink.*

LOWRY:
Bloody right. God, I'm sorry you're seeing me in this
condition. Look, I've got an idea. Let's call Jan, and
meet her for lunch together.

AIKEN:
Are you up to it?

LOWRY:
Feeling marvellous, now. I know this is a blasted
nuisance and all...but could you help me out? My
hand's a bit unsteady. A shave, maybe. Bit of a clean
up. Don't want her to see me like this, do we?

AIKEN:
I daresay we can get some of that grime off you, sure.

> *LOWRY sits down in a chair as AIKEN gathers up a
> metal bowl, towel and French straight razor.*

LOWRY:

Look here, this split-up's just temporary. We've done it before. We're like that.

AIKEN:

What's she doing now?

LOWRY: *chuckling*

Touch of the same old thing, if you catch my meaning.

AIKEN: *sadly*

Yes. I think I do.

LOWRY:

Actually, Conrad, I can't really blame her. She's discussed it. Quite openly. She's quite right. I haven't been...you know...much good for a while. *Beat.* A copywriter. This one's a copywriter or something. I haven't met him, but she talks about him a lot, so I guess it's okay for her.

AIKEN:

How about another snort? I can't shave you with your head bobbing around like that.

LOWRY takes a long pull on the mickey.

LOWRY:

Feeling steadier already. *Pause.* Conrad...?

AIKEN:

Yep?

LOWRY looks at him sadly, but finds it difficult to speak. He makes a sound of attempted speech and halts.

Yes, Malcolm? What's the problem?

LOWRY makes another attempt, and is finally able to frame it. He seems close to tears.

LOWRY:

For God's sake don't pity me. I'll kill you if you pity
me.

> *AIKEN looks at him, pauses, and finally shakes his head.*
> *He continues shaving him.*

AIKEN:

No.   *Beat.*   No. I can't pity you, Malc. I'll give
you a lift. My marriage is down the pipes too.

LOWRY: *cheerfully*

Really?

AIKEN:

Kaput! Or well on the road.

LOWRY:

I'm not surprised, you know.

AIKEN:

You vulgar little sod! This is really cheering you up,
isn't it?

LOWRY: *amused*

Misery loves company, old bird.

AIKEN:

Okay, misery. I'll really make your day. Not too long
ago, I tried to kill myself.

LOWRY:

I can't imagine it!

AIKEN:

What? My attempting it, or failing to succeed?

LOWRY:

For once, I think you've got a bigger scar than me.
What happened?

AIKEN:
>I sent Clarissa off to the pictures...locked myself in the kitchen, and turned on the gas. Unfortunately...or fortunately, depending on your perspective...she'd seen the bloody second feature, came home early and...just pulled me out. Unconscious. But still kicking.

LOWRY:
>Women spoil everything, don't they?

AIKEN:
>You'd think they could find two damn first-run features and put them on the same bill!   *Beat.*   Funny thing about women. They can't stand to see anything die.

LOWRY:
>Unless, of course, they kill it themselves.   *Beat.* Oh, Jesus, Conrad. It's so good to see you again. My God!

>*Blackout.*

Scene Three

Restaurant in New York—the same day.

The screens suggest the interior of a sophisticated New York restaurant in the mid-30s.

AIKEN sits alone at a table waiting.

JAN GABRIEL approaches from behind him, her heels clicking on the floor. She is dressed to kill.

AIKEN:
>   Hello, Jan.

JAN:
>   Hi, Conrad.

AIKEN:
>   I could tell it was you.

JAN:
>   What is it, darling, my aura or my perfume?

AIKEN:
>   I find it hard to believe that odour of destruction is perfume.

JAN:
>   Ouch! Still oozing charm, aren't we? Where is he?

AIKEN:
>   He stopped to buy flowers for you.

JAN:
>   Over your dead body, I bet.

AIKEN:
>   I suggested a Venus Flytrap.   *Beat.*   Darling.

JAN:
>   I'm not to blame. He's doing this to himself.

AIKEN:
>   You don't seem to be helping very much.

JAN:
>   That's damn unfair! You don't know what it's been like.

AIKEN:
>   And you do! From what I hear, you left him a month after you married him. Why did you do it in the first place?

JAN:

All the usual reasons. A whirlwind romance. He was brilliant, witty, charming and exciting. As only Malcolm can be when he's in top form. He bowled me over. *Beat.* I'm talking about love, not sex.

AIKEN:

Love?! *Beat.* I was very wrong about you, Jan. As an actress you might have had a very promising career.

JAN:

I didn't expect you to understand.

AIKEN:

Frankly, no. Is it love that guides you into the arms of whatever unqualified cocktail sausage you're currently stepping out with? Or is it love that prompts you to sit down and parade out your sordid little affairs, scene by bloody scene? Along with, let's not forget, the endearing facts of the poor bastard's sexual failings! Is this your idea of love?

JAN:

I suppose you'll say it's guilt.

AIKEN:

You said it.

JAN:

Conrad, dear...don't you feel just a teensy bit guilty yourself? I mean, don't you feel a twinge of irony? YOU lecturing ME on love and fidelity?

AIKEN:

That's not the bloody point!

JAN:

It is the bloody point. You sit there like a damn church elder, judging me...when we both know that you've been in and out of more bedrooms than the tooth fairy. *Beat.* You're smiling.

AIKEN:

I'm damn well not smiling!

JAN:

You make me puke! It's okay in your little boy's club to talk dirty, giggle and screw like rabbits. But let a woman try it, and she's suddenly immoral and insensitive, and a bitch to boot!!

AIKEN:

Let's not drag our feelings into it, Jan. We're talking about Malcolm. We both know he's not like us.

JAN:

That's why I love him. *Beat.* Dear God! He's a twenty-six-year-old terminal alcoholic! He's killing himself. I can't stand by and watch it! I can't go a week without seeing him. Bringing him out to lunch...trying to convince him.

AIKEN:

I'm having a hell of a time believing you.

JAN:

I don't give a tinker's damn if you do! I just care about him.

AIKEN: *studying her*
You puzzle me.

JAN:

I shouldn't. We're very much alike, Conrad. Survivors at any price. Malcolm's the puzzle. I don't know why he's doing this to himself. *Pause.* Can't you do something for him? You're the great teacher and father, aren't you?

AIKEN:

Not any more, I'm afraid. *Beat.* He's taking a long time. The florist is just down the block.

JAN: *amused, sadly*
You surprise me. You haven't guessed yet?

AIKEN:

How could I be so stupid!

JAN:

Those flowers are now highballs of cheap gin.

AIKEN:
Damn!!

JAN:

You have to watch him all the time. I know the drill. As you come down the road, he picks out some innocent reason to get off on his own. And he's gone. My first lesson about alcoholics. Even dead drunk, they're sharp as tacks.

AIKEN:
What can we do now?

JAN:

Well! You'll order a martini for me...one for yourself. We'll relax and yack about old times. And when the streets are cooler, we'll go look for him. We'll find him. I always do. *Beat.* Have a drink, Conrad. I'm an expert at this. Believe me.

AIKEN:

I should never have gone to see him.

JAN:

That's the second lesson. He lives by making others feel responsible for him. Like a child.

AIKEN:

Like a child.

JAN:

He got the money off you for the flowers, I'll bet.

AIKEN:

For the flowers.

JAN:

He certainly saw you coming, OLD BIRD. Well now. Let's start again. Hi, Conrad. Come on. Now you say: "I knew it was you." And I say: "Is it my aura, or my perfume." Come on, Conrad...OLD BIRD.

Blackout.

Musical Bridge: Opening of "Guadalajara."

Scene Four

Living-room, Lowry's house, Cuernavaca, Mexico—1937.

LOWRY enters with ED BURRA and AIKEN behind him carrying suitcases. Both are withered by the heat, and BURRA is visibly off-colour.

LOWRY: *calling out*
    Jan? Jan? *to others* Drop your bags down
    anywhere. I'll find something to cool you off.

    *AIKEN and BURRA look at one another and let go of
    their bags in unison.*

AIKEN:
    Sweet Jesus! You could fry a steak out on that street!

BURRA:
    Alas! The Mexicans insist on using kitchens. I'm sure
    the streets are ten times more sanitary!

LOWRY:
    Off the top, I can offer you water or beer. I'd take the
    beer. It's got a few hundred less squiggly things in it.

AIKEN:
    Nothing for Ed. I think his lunch is revolting on him.
    I'll have a beer.

BURRA:
    God! I just remembered the Alamo. I'm of the opinion
    the Mexicans weren't invading Texas at all. They were
    just screaming to get out of this damned country!

LOWRY:
    When your stomachs are flexed up, you can try the
    tequila. It'll help kill the bacteria in the beer.

    LOWRY exits after giving a beer to AIKEN.

    *In the silence that follows, BURRA stares accusingly at
    AIKEN.*

AIKEN:
    Just a couple of weeks, Ed. It won't be that bad.

BURRA:

    Conrad! It's beyond me why I let you talk me into this. We've been in this inferno barely a day. I've got botulism and a terminal heat rash, and I'm rapidly losing weight from both ends! I'm surrounded by leering banditos who'd strangle a bus load of nuns for the price of a drink...and we've got a host in there who thinks gin and vermouth is a two course meal. *Beat.* And you say it won't be that bad! God help me!

    LOWRY returns with JAN.

JAN:

    Conrad! What a pleasant surprise.

    JAN embraces AIKEN.

AIKEN:

    You remember Ed Burra, Jan. Granada, I think.

JAN:

    Of course. Nice to see you again. How are you?

BURRA:

    Quite...tense.

JAN:

    Nothing a good meal and sunshine won't cure, I hope. *Beat.* Whatever brought you to Cuernavaca?

BURRA:

    We came to enjoy one of the country's great attractions. A quick Mexican divorce.

    LOWRY and JAN stare at BURRA in surprise.

Oh God! Not me! I'm Conrad's witness. He's getting married again.

LOWRY:

Splendid! Congratulations, old boy. Who's the lucky lady?

JAN:

At a guess, I'd say Clarissa.

LOWRY:

Jan! That's a bit thick!

JAN:

Oh, he knows I'm pulling his leg. Don't you, Conrad?

AIKEN:

You don't know her, Malc. Fine lady. A painter as it happens.

LOWRY:

Look, Jan...with Conrad turning up like this, and so forth...do you think perhaps...?

JAN:

Before you ask. No. It's all arranged. I can't cancel it.

LOWRY:

Not cancel it. Can you postpone it?

JAN:

No, and please drop it.   *Beat.*   You'll have to excuse me, all. I've got an afternoon bus to catch, and I'm still not packed.

AIKEN:

Yes. Of course.

JAN exits, and LOWRY calls loudly after her.

LOWRY:

Jan? Please, Jan!

AIKEN:

> Sorry, Malc. Maybe we shouldn't have dropped in without warning.

LOWRY:

> Good Lord, no. This is a weekend trip she's had in the works for some time. *Beat.* Look, I'll be right back. Make yourselves at home.

BURRA: *calling out*

> Excuse me, Lowry. Where's your powder room?

LOWRY:

> Powder room? *Beat.* Oh! The shithouse! Through the back at the side of the house. But watch yourself in there, old chap. The scorpions take shelter in it, midday.

BURRA:

> Sweet Jesus in the morning!!

> *LOWRY exits.*

LOWRY: *calling out*

> Jan! Jan!

BURRA:

> Oh, Conrad! Let's get the hell out of here! It's like Dagwood and Blondie with real blood!!

AIKEN:

> I have a feeling this isn't an unusual day for them.

BURRA:

> What is it with these two?! I thought you told me she'd already packed it in.

AIKEN:

> Christ! Don't ask me. They got together again, and came down here. God knows why!

BURRA:

> So I want to know. Thrill my wasted body with the truth. *Beat.* What do you think of your budding genius now?

AIKEN:

> Come on, Ed.

BURRA:

> He's a skid-row derelict with an English accent. I'm sure the most creative thing he's done in the past five years is puke down his shirt front!

AIKEN:

> You're a cynical bastard. You know that?

BURRA:

> I'm a realist born in wedlock. And it's about time you faced the truth. I've told you about this one from the beginning.

AIKEN:

> You think he fooled me.

BURRA:

> You fooled yourself.

AIKEN:

> Is there anything in this world you believe in, Ed? Really?

BURRA:

> Yes. I believe Santa Claus is a lie...happy endings are trite...and you can't make a silk Tolstoy out of a drunk's ear! *Beat.* Conrad, old duck... bird!...whatever the hell it is he calls you! You can't seem to accept things as they are, can you?

AIKEN:

> To be absolutely frank with you, I never liked things as they are.

BURRA:

There you are! A romantic dribbling delusions from
every orifice.   *Beat.*   Oh God! Why did I use that
expression?

AIKEN:

"I too have heard the sea sound in strange waters."

BURRA:

Good for you.

AIKEN:

Malcolm wrote that to me once. About a thousand years
ago.

BURRA:

A deathless line. I'm sure it will echo through eternity.

AIKEN:

Come off it, Ed. With your...well-honed Oscar Wilde
impersonations. You're a bigger romantic than any of
us. Just a more disillusioned one, that's all.

BURRA:

And at the moment, old friend, you're disillusioning me
most. You still believe he's a great genius of promise?
Well, do you?

AIKEN: *quietly*
No. No, I don't.

BURRA:

You still believe he can write the great novel?

AIKEN:
No.

BURRA:

You have no belief in him at all?

AIKEN:
No. NO!! What do you want me to say?

BURRA:
Welcome back to the world.

> *JAN comes back into the the room carrying a suitcase. She pauses uncomfortably, and BURRA starts out of the room.*

JAN:
Well...?

BURRA: *suffering an attack*
Why is this being inflicted on me?   *He starts out of the room.*   If it's my fate to die cruelly alone in a Mexican toilet, I want you to suffer as I have, Conrad. When they carry me out, as a tribute to romantics everywhere...DRINK THE LOCAL WATER!!

> *BURRA quickly exits, and JAN calls after him.*

JAN: *calling*
There's a broom near the back door, Ed. You can use it to sweep the scorpions off the wall.

BURRA: *off-stage*
Oh God! Help me!

> *JAN and AIKEN pause after BURRA leaves, uncomfortable with each other.*

JAN:
Malcolm will be out in a while. He's taking a nap.

AIKEN:
What's going on, Jan?

JAN: *shrugging*
Not much. I'm going away for the weekend. I'm sorry it came at the same time as your visit.

AIKEN:

I see.

JAN:

Don't look at me like that!

AIKEN:

Look at you like what?

JAN:

Yes, damn it! It's the same thing! He's still the same, and I'm still the same. I'm not going to play mother to a hopeless drunk any more. I'm not going to sacrifice the one life I have to further Art. Fuck Art!!

AIKEN:

Jan?

JAN:

I've been fighting with Malcolm. I'm a little jumpy. He's not in there sleeping. He's swilling down a bottle. It's his way of punishing me. Brilliant, eh?

AIKEN:

You're off to spend a weekend with someone else?

JAN:

Not SOMEONE. A lover. It's a difficult word, isn't it? But let's get the order straight. He's not drinking because I'm going to see a lover. It's the other way around.

AIKEN:

Why did you come back to him?

JAN:

He's a weak man! You have no idea how powerful a weak man can be! He lives by making others feel responsible for him. He turns love into guilt. And I'm

sick of feeling guilty! *Beat.* I leave, worry about
him, and come back. Over and over. I just hope to hell
I have the strength to stay away this time.

AIKEN:
We all have to escape.

JAN:
Escape!! You son of a bitch!! I can't tell you how
grateful I am for your words of encouragement.
Beat. You know, I don't know whether to envy or
pity you. Somehow you've managed to escape it all.
Love. Guilt. Even pain.

AIKEN:
No. No, I haven't. *Beat.* Come on, you're
going to miss your bus.

> *JAN starts toward the door. LOWRY quickly enters and
> overtakes her. He's been timing this moment. He carries a
> small package in his hands.*

LOWRY:
Hold on, Jan. I nearly forgot this.

> *He holds out the package to her. JAN takes it, avoiding
> eye contact with him.*

JAN:
What's this?

LOWRY:
Your birthday. It's tomorrow. I didn't
forget. *Beat.* Aren't you going to open it?

JAN:
I've got to go. I'll open it later.

LOWRY:
It's the silver earrings you liked so much. I. went out
and got them this morning.

JAN:
> Goodbye, Conrad.

> *JAN turns and exits. LOWRY turns back to AIKEN.*

LOWRY:
> Good Lord! You're drinkless! You must forgive me, old bird. A little tequila? It's all I have. Ghastly stuff, but it helps what ails.

AIKEN:
> Sure. Why not.

LOWRY:
> He's an engineer or something. Up in the silver mines north of here.

AIKEN:
> She told you that?

LOWRY:
> Of course. She tells me everything.

AIKEN:
> Doesn't it bother you, Malc?

LOWRY:
> I'd say that's the general idea, wouldn't you?

AIKEN:
> Yes. No. Christ! I don't know. Make it a stiff tequila, would you.

> *LOWRY crosses the room with a glass and a bottle of tequila.*

LOWRY:
> Supply's down, I'm afraid. Finish this off. I'll take a stroll over to the local cantina for replacements.

AIKEN:
> I'll go with you.

LOWRY:
> I'd rather go alone, if you don't mind.

AIKEN:
> You're coming right back?

LOWRY:
> Immediately.

AIKEN:
> I don't believe you, Malc.

> *LOWRY turns and looks at him.*

LOWRY:
> I didn't ask you to believe me, OLD BIRD.

> *LOWRY exits.*

> *Lights Dim.*

> *Musical Bridge: A romantic version of "Via Con Dios."*

Scene Five

The same, later that evening.

AIKEN looks after LOWRY, and then moves to the table. He hefts the bottle of tequila, pours a drink, quickly swallows it, and then sees the old taropatch on the table. It is stringless. He picks it up and studies it, remembering what once had been. He notices LOWRY's manuscript on

105

the table. He picks it up and studies it as he reaches for another tequila. Gradually he is drawn away from the tequila, to study the manuscript more closely. He scans line after line, page after page. He is finally transfixed by it. He is mortified, confused, elated. AIKEN is in awe. He shakes his head, and moves his lips as he reads over a passage. Finally he raises his head and calls upstairs.

AIKEN:
Good God! Good God! Oh my God!   *pausing to shout aloud*   Ed! Ed! I hope you can hear me. I hope you never shit in peace again. You were wrong, you cynical bastard! I was wrong! He's done it! I don't know how, but that booze-sodden, beautiful ugly child has done it!   *lowering his voice*   He's done it.

> *AIKEN collapses into a chair. The full import of the feat is striking him. He is out-written, and he must confront it.*

It's not a question of gifts. It's a question of theft. Theft! How?! How could he possibly do this to me? Why? Why?   *shouting*   DAMN IT! WHY!

> *AIKEN sits back in the chair in silence, more than a little dazed.*

> *LOWRY enters weaving, drunk, with two bottles of mescal. He is in a dangerous, unpredictable mood.*

LOWRY:
See? Two virgins. Mescal. The real stuff. Muy correcto! Where is everybody?

AIKEN:
Ed's gone to bed.

LOWRY:

Oh. Yes. Quite forgot. Jan's... *He whistles.*
Vamosa! *Beat.* Well, via con bloody dios to her,
eh? Hear that? Scorpions. Real. They get under the
tiles. Very active just before the rains hit. And the ants.

AIKEN:

The what?

LOWRY:

The ants. You forgot the ants. They'll take your eyes
out while you sleep, if you give them half a chance.
Now look here, old boy. Know it might seem the pit of
the earth to you. But it has a beauty. Unearthly. You
have no idea how truly and perfectly lovely it is.

AIKEN:

I'm afraid I can't agree with you on that.

LOWRY:

Along with a couple of other things. My manuscript.
The great masterpiece in progress. I see you've been
reading it. So far you've said nothing. With you, I
regard that as a bad sign.

AIKEN:

"Under the Volcano." I think it's brilliant.

LOWRY:

A drunken babble, eh? The verbal pyrotechnics of a
sodden mind?

AIKEN:

I think I was hoping it would be.

LOWRY

Well...spit it out, old bird. Let's have the benefit of all
that grey wisdom of yours. Too much ebb and a
conspicuous dearth of flow?

AIKEN:
    It's over. The time for teaching is long passed. Okay?

LOWRY: *after a long pause*
    I see.   *Beat.*   Clouds over Popocateptl. It'll rain
    shortly. Comes down in bloody torrents.

AIKEN:
    Why did you do this?

LOWRY:
    Funny thing is it never changes anything. Next day it's
    just as hot and dry as if it never rained at all.

AIKEN:
    Why did you do this to me?

LOWRY:
    Demons! Exorcising the bastards! Will that do?

AIKEN: *exploding*
    Not your artistic motivation, you insufferable drunk!
    Your theft! You've got images of mine in there...ideas of
    mine I discussed with you years ago!

    LOWRY studies him drunkenly, and then chuckles.

LOWRY:
    Exactly.

AIKEN:
    What the hell's that supposed to mean? EXACTLY?!

LOWRY:
    You've done nothing about them, have you?

AIKEN:
    That's hardly the point...!

LOWRY:
> Anyway, don't take on so. It's only a couple of minor themes...used in a couple of places, that's all.

AIKEN:
> They weren't minor to me, and you damn well know it!

LOWRY:
> Yes. It would appear your GREAT themes are serviceable only in minor, secondary roles, old boy.

AIKEN: *astounded*
> DAMN!   *He paces, searching for words.*   Damn! Malcolm...why are you...? DAMN! WHY?!

LOWRY:
> Oh come on. This is what you wanted all along. You planned this.

AIKEN:
> This is lunatic. I'll talk to you when you're sober.

> *AIKEN is about to leave, but LOWRY moves drunkenly and dangerously across the room and slings him back into a chair.*

LOWRY:
> In...vino...sanitas...You're nearly dead. Let's finish the job.

AIKEN:
> I'm not going to fight with you.

> *In a drunken, amused, and almost detached fashion, LOWRY glares at him unsteadily, then gets a glass and pours some of the mescal into it from one of the bottles. He passes the glass to AIKEN while he retains the bottle in his hand.*

> *AIKEN takes the glass cautiously.*

LOWRY holds the bottle out in a toast.

LOWRY:
A toast. To the inevitable order. To death and betrayal. *Beat.* Say it! Death and betrayal.

AIKEN glares back at him, then he takes the glass and spills the contents slowly onto the floor.

LOWRY bends down, and licks falling drops from the upturned glass that AIKEN is holding. AIKEN turns his face away in horror and disgust.

LOWRY takes the glass from him and hurls it to the floor. It smashes.

LOWRY then takes the nearly full bottle of mescal and swallows it all down at once. He stands dazed afterwards, and lets the bottle slip from his hand and fall to the floor. He walks unsteadily back to one of the chairs and sinks into it, slightly dazed.

My God! My God!...isn't reality loathsome? Utterly loathsome.

AIKEN:
That, at any rate, I can share with you.

LOWRY: *turning on him*
You knew...when you first saw me...you knew, every creative thought you ever had would find a better home in me. I was younger. Stronger. More committed. And the waning father breathed his spirit into the waxing son, didn't he? "Consciousness"...how often did you tell me that?..."Consciousness warrants the ultimate sacrifice."

AIKEN:
And I'm to become the sacrifice, am I?

110

LOWRY:

No damn fear! I'm the sacrifice, Conrad! Me! You
made sure I would give everything for my art. My
happiness. My life. God!...even my sanity!
Beat. Faustus...damned to perdition for my
knowledge...Oh Christ, save me! Save me!....SAVE
ME!!

AIKEN stands and tries to approach him.

AIKEN:

Malc? I never suggested....

*LOWRY turns on him suddenly, grabs him, and throws
him onto the floor. LOWRY's manuscript that AIKEN
has been holding is thrown into the air and spreads across
the stage. LOWRY gets down astride AIKEN and pins
him to the floor.*

LOWRY: *quietly, coldly*

We know the price I've paid, OLD BIRD. And now
yours. We know that too, don't we? I've absorbed you.
I've killed you finally, drained from you all the
knowledge you were unable to use...for lack of courage
or consciousness. Or, even, perversely enough, by your
own design. Because, after it's over...and you've always
known it as much as you feared it...I will be the one
they remember. I am as much their tragic flaw as I am
yours. And I will make art of it.

*LOWRY stands, puts the overturned chairs back into
position, and then crosses back to AIKEN. He offers him
his hand to help him stand. AIKEN backs away, fearful
of his mood, but LOWRY laughs inanely. AIKEN takes
his hand, but as he rises, LOWRY, drunk now from the
mescal, falls on his knees. AIKEN helps him to his feet
and drags him to a chair. He then seats himself in a chair
facing LOWRY.*

111

AIKEN: *chuckling*
Oh God! We're like the two bears up the tree. Ah...you
know, when I was a child, in Savannah...there was this
man...from the circus, I guess he was.... He had these
two dancing bears...with these ridiculous looking little
hats...at the end of these chains.   *Aiken sees the old
taropatch and picks it up.*   Your old ukulele.   *Beat.*
No. What did you call it?

LOWRY:
Taropatch.

AIKEN: *nodding*
No strings.

LOWRY:
Been like that for a long time. But it's still good to hold.

AIKEN moves his hands on it strumming it soundlessly.

AIKEN:
So. The bears. See my father was well known in town,
so the man used to come over to our house once a year,
and have the bears dance for us...a private show in front
of our verandah. Well, this one year, my father said to
the man: "What'll happen if you take the chain off?"
And the man said: "Nothing. They're quite tame."
And to prove it, he took the chain off one of the bears.
We had this huge, old oak tree...   *Beat.*   old oak
tree...massive. Anyway, damned if the bear didn't...

LOWRY: *enchanted*
...right up the old oak tree.

AIKEN:
And he wouldn't come down. The man cajoled,
pleaded, shouted, begged, but he wouldn't come down.
Finally, he said: "I know what'll bring him down...."

LOWRY:
The other bear, of course.

AIKEN:
> Of course. He's better trained. Older. More sensible. He'll respond to orders. So he took the chain of the other bear and zoom...

LOWRY:
> ...right up the old oak tree.

AIKEN:
> You know what happened when he called the second bear to come down?

LOWRY:
> He wouldn't come, I'll wager.

AIKEN: *laughing*
> The two of them stayed up there as happy as clams.   *Beat.*   Maybe they're still up there, yet.

> *LOWRY slips out of his chair in a drunken stupor, then crawls about the floor gathering up the pages from his manuscript. He grips them to himself—as many as he can gather—and crawls under the table. He assumes a fetal position and passes out.*

> *AIKEN stands and regards him with a mixture of sadness and disgust.*

Goodnight. Goodnight disgrace.

> *AIKEN comes forward and the lights fade on LOWRY.*

Scene Six

Rest home, Savannah, Georgia—1973

As the NURSE wheels his chair in and helps him on with his old bathrobe, AIKEN becomes an old man of 85 again.

The NURSE exits, as AIKEN gazes out over the audience.

AIKEN:
Under the Volcano is a work of genius. It really is.   *quoting*   "A changeable shot-silk sun-shot medium of infinite flexibility." That's what I wrote for the book jacket. Whatever the hell that mouthful of bullshit is supposed to mean! I think I always overdid my adjectives. Was always damn well ebbing when I should have been damn well flowing. Hate my writing.   *Beat.*   I saw him once more, you know. Twenty years later in New York. He was so pissed he couldn't even talk to me. Just bubbled saliva from his mouth and hummed jazz tunes of some kind. *Beat.*   He'd been drinking aftershave lotion.   *Beat.*   Never did write much of any consequence after *Volcano*. Damned if I know how he did that. But I loved him. I really did. It was the last time I ever saw him. Three years later he died in England. An overdose of barbiturates. But they called it death by misadventure.... Thank God it's finally over. Now I can get some peace.

The NURSE enters, carrying a bowl of tapioca.

You know I don't want you to tell people here who I am. If they ask, just tell 'em I'm a crazy old man come home to die.

He sees the bowl that she is carrying.

NURSE:
It's tapioca, Mr. Aiken.

AIKEN studies the contents of the bowl and looks up at the NURSE, his face lighting up.

AIKEN:
Ohmigod! It's Thursday!   *Beat.*   Nurse?

The lights fade on the figures on the stage as the screen slips into the final images.

AIKEN motions for the NURSE to lean down. He kisses her, and they freeze in position, with LOWRY still motionless under the table.

Music: "Vincent."